CAPABILITY]
IN
NORFOLK

Edited by

SALLY BATE

NORFOLK GARDENS TRUST

ISBN 978-0-9556728-5-9

This book is available direct from the:

Norfolk Gardens Trust

via the 'Get in Touch' page on our website:

www.norfolkgt.org.uk

or from

The Editor

Tel: 0788 190 7735

sally@bate.vianw.co.uk

Printed and bound in Great Britain by

Barnwell Print, Ltd, Aylsham, Norfolk, NR11 6SU

WORLD LAND TRUST™

www.carbonbalancedpaper.com
CBP0004460908161403

By using Carbon Balanced Paper through the World Land Trust on this publication we have offset 473kg of Carbon & preserved 40sqm of critically threatened tropical forests.

Carbon Balanced Paper. One of the most sustainable forms of communication that will reduce your carbon foot print and promote CSR. www.carbonbalancedpaper.com

CONTENTS

PREFACE

This book celebrates the 300th anniversary of the birth of Lancelot 'Capability' Brown on 30 August with a study of his work in Norfolk, illustrated with 135 stunning illustrations. It coincides with numerous exhibitions, publications and events held nationwide to celebrate the life, works and influence of a man often referred to as the father of landscape architecture. His best known surviving landscapes include the parks and gardens at Blenheim, Burghley, Chatsworth, Alnwick and Highclere. Much has been written and recorded at famous locations such as these, however, Brown worked at over 240 sites in his career and a number of his lesser known landscapes have not survived or remain relatively unrecorded.

In 2013 eleven members of the Norfolk Gardens Trust formed a research group with shared interests in gardens, landscape art and history. They decided to investigate Brown's three Norfolk sites at Kimberley, Langley and Melton Constable, all currently in private ownership. Soon it became apparent that the group needed advice on recording and interpreting landscapes on such a big scale and so they enlisted the help of Professor Tom Williamson at the University of East Anglia. He has provided a venue to hold meetings, helped with editing and standardising the text and most importantly written chapters that introduce Lancelot Brown to the reader and describe other sites in Norfolk associated with him. He concludes the book with a brief account setting Brown's landscapes amongst the many other parks established in Norfolk during the eighteenth century.

The Norfolk Gardens Trust Research Group is excited to be publishing this book to coincide with 'Capability' Brown's tercentenary celebrations and to bring to print for the first time his three plans and one detailed contract for Kimberley, Langley and Melton Constable (Chapters 2, 3 and 4). In order to examine Brown's proposals and determine how many of them were carried out, visits to the parks took place alongside archival research in private and public collections, as well as the Norfolk Record Office. At the beginning of these three chapters the authors have given an account of the people, historical events and landscape changes that shaped the parks before the 1760s, in order to understand what Brown saw, and had to work with, when he and his men arrived on site. Following analysis of his documents, as well as countless other contemporary descriptions, plans and illustrations, each chapter details Brown's proposals and records which of these features, buildings and design elements still exist today. The chapters conclude with a summary of changes the parks underwent in the nineteenth and twentieth centuries, some of which have masked Brown's earlier work.

None of this research would have possible without the generosity and hospitality of the parks' owners, who allowed our researchers to record, measure and explore most of the areas covered by Brown's landscape 'improvements', as well as giving them access to their personal archives. The Norfolk Gardens Trust Research Group is enormously grateful to the organisations and individuals who have helped them to study and reproduce the images printed in this book. Although full acknowledgements are given in the next section, special mention must be made of two photographers. Mike Page has very kindly given the research group eight of his spectacular aerial photographs, which are the only way to appreciate fully the scale of Brown's landscapes. Roger Last has also been invaluable to the project, by producing clear photographic images of documents and paintings, despite some being located in challenging situations!

The editor and authors of the book would like pay tribute to their families and friends for their patience and support during such an absorbing time, while they amassed the information, worked on several drafts of the text, tracked down images and gained reproduction permissions before assembling the book. Also they would like to convey their thanks and appreciation to their copy-editor Mary Worthington, their indexer Sarah Harrison and to Richard Pryor and the staff at Barnwell Print in Aylsham.

The Norfolk Gardens Trust (formed in 1988) promotes the conservation, restoration, knowledge and enjoyment of gardens and designed landscapes in the county. At the time of writing the Trust has over 500 members, and organises talks, garden visits and study days. This is the second book the Trust has produced, following the much acclaimed gazetteer *Norfolk Gardens and Designed Landscapes* published in 2013, and it is now pleased to share with readers the recent findings about Lancelot 'Capability' Brown and his work in Norfolk.

Norfolk Gardens Trust Research Group – August 2016

Sally Bate	Marcia Fenwick	Rachel Savage
Sue Brown	Bob Greef	Tom Williamson
Pamela Clark	Andrew Fuller	Judith Wilson
Janet Ede	Kate Minnis	Peter Woodrow

ACKNOWLEDGEMENTS

The Norfolk Gardens Trust would like to thank the following people and organisations for their help and support in writing this book:

The Buxton Family of Kimberley Hall, the Gawn Family of Melton Constable and the Governors, Headmaster and Julian Long (Estate Operations Manager) of Langley School.

For sharing their knowledge and own research:

Professor Tom Williamson, Dr Jon Gregory, Dr Sarah Spooner and Dr Andrew Macnair of the University of East Anglia. Also Dr Patsy Dallas, Dr David Brown and Dr John Maddison.

For help in providing digital images or allowing us to photograph paintings, maps and other documents:

Trustees of Burghley House, Duke of Marlborough and the Blenheim Estate, Duke of Beaufort and the Badminton Estate, Marquis of Lansdowne and the Bowood Estate, Earl of Leicester and trustees of the Holkham Estate, Earl and Countess Ferrers, Sir Nicholas and Lady Bacon, Lord and Lady Walpole, Ordnance Survey, The British Library, staff of the Norfolk Record Office, Norfolk County Council – Library and Information Service and Planning Department, Royal Institute of British Architects, National Trust Images and Seaton Delaval Hall NT (Northumberland), Anna Smith and the Council of the National Army Museum, Mark Bills and Sophie Woods of Gainsborough's House (Sudbury), Megan Dennis, Lucy McNeill and Lauren Ephithite at Norwich Museums Service (Gressenhall Farm and Workhouse, Norwich Castle Museum and Art Gallery), National Portrait Gallery (London), Bodleian Library (Oxford), Clive Marks at the Government Art Collection, Clare Broomfield at the Historic England Archive, Tate Art Galleries (London), Toledo Museum (Ohio), Huntington Art Collection (San Marino, California), Mike Page Aerial Photography, Christine Hiskey, Nadine Hepper, Roger Last, Stephen Fenny, Audrey Young, Peter Prideaux-Brune, Colin Shearer and Frances Kirkpatrick.

For assistance with research, surveying, technical support, copy-editing and proofreading:

NGT Research Group, staff at Hussey Knights (Norwich), Mary Worthington, Danny Bate, Richard Colman, Richard Deller, Matthew and Anne Hutton, Anthea Taigel, Tony Bate, Yvonne Mallett, Tony Clark and Sarah Harrison.

CHAPTER 1   INTRODUCING LANCELOT BROWN

Lancelot 'Capability' Brown (1716 – 1783).
Studio of Sir Nathaniel Dance-Holland Bt. R.A. (©Burghley House)

This short book is a celebration of the parks and gardens created in Norfolk by Lancelot 'Capability' Brown, unquestionably the most famous of all English landscape designers. Brown flourished in the middle and later decades of the eighteenth century and, together with less famous contemporaries, was responsible for bringing to fruition a move towards 'natural' landscaping which had begun some decades earlier. Walled gardens, avenues and geometric planting – everything straight, symmetrical and regular – were swept away from around the homes of the wealthy, and in their place more irregular landscapes were created – 'landscape parks', as they are often known. These comprised wide prospects of uninterrupted turf, scattered rather sparsely with individual trees and clumps, and surrounded in whole or part by a perimeter woodland belt. Where circumstances allowed, Brown provided a lake of serpentine or irregular form, and sometimes an ornamental building, such as a classical temple, or two.[1]   Although highly structured gardens were removed from around the main facades of a mansion, pleasure grounds of some kind remained, although they were now usually separated from the grazed parkland not by a wall but by a sunken fence or ha-ha. Brown, and to a lesser extent other designers, usually laid out numerous serpentine drives and rides through the parkland, often running in and out of the perimeter belt.   The landscapes created by Brown were supposedly so 'natural' in appearance, and so English in character, that Horace Walpole believed that 'he will be least remembered: so closely did he copy nature that his works will be mistaken for it'.[2]

Lancelot Brown was born in 1716 at Kirkharle in Northumberland. It is sometimes suggested that his origins were lowly, but everything is relative. His father was a prosperous yeoman farmer, his brother John married the daughter of the local squire, Sir William Lorraine, and Brown himself attended the local grammar school until he was sixteen – a sure sign of a broadly middle-class background. After he had completed his schooling he worked on Sir William's estate for seven years and probably learnt much about estate management and forestry. In 1739 he moved south, first to work at Grimsthorpe in Lincolnshire and subsequently on a number of Midland estates, where he designed ornamental lakes.[3] In 1742 he took up a post at Stowe in Buckinghamshire.   Here Richard Temple, first Viscount Cobham, had been creating complex and elaborate gardens for over 20 years with a succession of talented architects and designers, including Charles Bridgeman, Sir John Vanbrugh, James Gibbs and William Kent.[4]   When Brown arrived on the scene Kent was busy laying out a novel section of the grounds, the 'Elysian Fields', a serpentine, irregular garden containing a large number of ornamental buildings (Figure 1).   Most of these conveyed – through their form, inscriptions, and relationship with other structures – political and philosophical messages. Brown continued this work and designed several buildings himself – the Temple of Concord and the Temple of Victory – something 'which raised him into some degree of estimation as an architect'.[5] His main role, however, was as clerk of works, and it was through this that he doubtless learnt the organisational skills which were to stand him in such good stead in later years.

Figure 1.
The 'Elysian Fields' at Stowe, largely laid out under the direction of William Kent in the 1730s and 1740s, as it survives today, still punctuated with ornamental buildings. (Photo: Jon Gregory)

Even while occupied at Stowe, Brown took on a number of commissions for friends of Lord Cobham. When Cobham died in 1749 Brown left and moved to Hammersmith near London, where he established himself as an independent designer of landscapes, and by 1760 he had undertaken perhaps 30 major commissions. Over the following two decades he became the leading designer in the country, a household name, 'the great Arbiter of British Taste';[6] and from 1764 he occupied the post of Master Gardener at Hampton Court and lived in a house in the Palace grounds. Such was the scale of his success that, when he died in 1783, Brown was the owner of a landed estate at Fenstanton in Huntingdonshire extending over more than 3,000 acres. By this time, he had probably worked on over 240 sites. The precise number is uncertain because only one of Brown's account books survives, listing a mere 19 commissions which were begun in the early 1760s, while his bank accounts (which exist for his entire career) omit many of the places he is known to have worked, payment having presumably been made

3

to him in other ways.[7] As we shall see, in Norfolk as elsewhere there are places where Brown's activities have been claimed, but contested. But, while undiscovered commissions doubtless still exist, there is no doubt that the vast majority of landscape parks created in England in the second half of the eighteenth century were in fact the work of other designers.

We must be careful not to exaggerate the originality of Brown's style, and the extent to which it represented a break with what had gone before. While he is often credited with having 'swept away' walled, geometric gardens, as intimated earlier the old formal styles had, in reality, been in retreat for decades. From the start of the eighteenth century the grounds of the most fashionable residences began to be laid out in a simpler manner than before, with plain grass lawns, gravel paths, and extensive woodland gardens – 'wildernesses' – containing paths which became ever more serpentine with the passing years. Through the 1720s and 1730s, individuals like Charles Bridgeman – who in Norfolk worked at Wolterton, Houghton, Gunton, and almost certainly at Blickling – developed a more extensive version of this stripped-down formality, embracing the parkland as much as the gardens, and increasingly dissolved the boundary between the two by replacing walls with a sunken fence.[8] By the 1730s large irregular lakes – a feature we often associate with Brown and his contemporaries – were already appearing at a number of places, including Wolterton and Holkham.[9] By the 1730s William Kent was laying out his irregular, serpentine gardens, and not only at Stowe. At Holkham, from the mid-1730s, he created – immediately below the south front of the hall, still then under construction – a novel area of gardens, surrounded by a winding path, completely lacking any formal symmetry, although as at Stowe set within a wider landscape of simplified geometry. It featured a 'serpentine river', an artificial hillock surmounted by the 'Seat on the Mount', and irregularly scattered trees, the whole composition strongly reminiscent of the paintings of classical scenes made by Claude Lorraine and Nicolas Poussin. These romantic portrayals of the Italian landscape were widely hung on the walls of fashionable houses (Figure 2).

At numerous places, through the 1740s, gardens with serpentine layouts were created which featured growing numbers of ornamental buildings: classical temples were now joined by gothic ruins, hermitages, Chinese pagodas and 'Turkish tents'.[10] Once again, these 'rococo' gardens (as historians now describe them) usually accompanied, rather than replaced, earlier grounds laid out in more regular and formal mode. Serpentine and irregular designs, gardens without walls, large

Figure 2.
Claude Lorraine, 'Landscape with Nymph and Satyr Dancing'. The landscapes created by William Kent were closely based on paintings like this, produced in the late seventeenth century by artists like Lorraine and Nicholas Poussin, of idealised Italian scenery, strewn with classical ruins. (Toledo Museum)

non-geometric lakes and romantic buildings were thus already familiar features in the grounds of the wealthy by the time that Brown began his career. Indeed, as early as 1739, the year he came south from Northumberland, one contributor to *The World* was able to ridicule the contemporary fashion for 'moving earth', and the way that 'a Serpentine River and a Wood are become the absolute Necessities of Life, without which a gentleman of the smallest fortune thinks he makes no Figure in the country'.[11]

There is another way in which Brown's originality can be exaggerated. His style did not appear, fully formed, at the start of his career. Instead it developed gradually, over time, and at no point can we say without reservation that he was ahead of the stylistic curve. He appears to have been one of a group of landscape gardeners who gradually developed a distinctive mode of simple and naturalistic design through the 1750s and 1760s. Brown was certainly the most financially successful, but his style was probably the style of the times, rather than something

5

unique or specific to him. His early works – at places like Ingestre in Staffordshire and Badminton in Gloucestershire – were no different from other elaborately serpentine gardens of the time[12] (Figure 3). They were often cluttered with buildings and still, in many cases, co-existed with geometric features. At Moor Park in Hertfordshire, for example, he laid out an extensive, 'naturalistic' pleasure ground to the east of the mansion – replacing a more formal, monumental design created a few years earlier by Charles Bridgeman – but apparently did nothing in the parkland beyond, which continued to be filled with a dense mesh of avenues.[13]

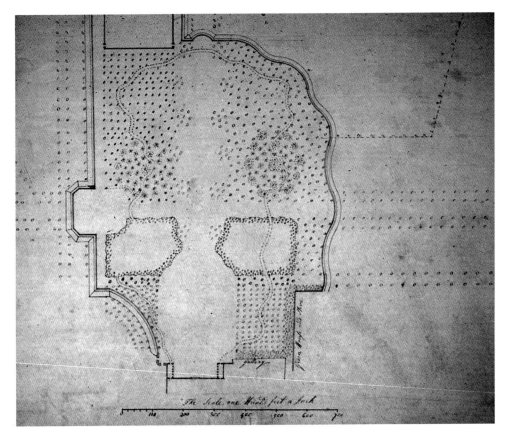

Figure 3.
Brown's design for the pleasure ground at Badminton, Gloucestershire, c.1752. Brown's early works were often still rather stiff and formal, like those of his contemporary designers. (By kind permission of the Duke of Beaufort and the Badminton Estate)

Much of his effort at this stage of his career went into the design of garden buildings, which were – as in other ornamental landscapes in this period – often numerous. At Temple Newsam in Yorkshire in the early 1760s he thus designed and built sham bridges, a rotunda, a menagerie, a cottage, a dairy and a grotto.[14] His planting of the pleasure grounds lying within the ha-ha was often complex and elaborate, as at Petworth in Sussex, where the planting list drawn up in 1753 includes: sweet bryony, honeysuckle, altheas, spirea, oriental colutea, bird cherry, 'double cherry', candleberry trees, butchers broom, ilex, sweet briar, double thorn, Persian jasmine, 'Virginian Sumacs', Virginia raspberry, tamarisks, American maples, sea buckthorn, 'trumpet flowers', roses, Portugal laurel, laburnums, lilacs, acacias and the roses 'Rosa Mundi', 'Maidens Blush, and 'York and Lancaster'.[15]

Yet Brown's art was developing fast and already, by the late 1750s, one of the key elements of his style was in place: the recurrent arrangement of mansion, looking down across smooth sloping turf, to an irregular or serpentine area of water. Other designers, such as Francis Richardson, were already doing something very similar. However, by this stage Brown was beginning to cream off the wealthiest clients, the kinds of individuals who had the money for such expensive improvements as levelling and lake-making, so that his compositions tend to feature this central *ensemble* more than most. He began to design on a grander and simpler scale, paying particular attention to drives and approaches, gradually reducing the numbers of ornamental buildings and relying on trees, water and the configuration of the natural topography to create landscapes of serpentine simplicity. Smooth and swelling landforms – their outlines suitably modified by excavation and earth-movement – were the key feature. By the early 1760s all the elements of Brown's style were firmly in place, including the multiplicity of gravelled drives and rides, the latter often weaving in and out of the perimeter wooded belt (Figure 4).

All this did not, as we shall see, mean that Brown ceased to pay attention to the gardens and shrubberies in the immediate vicinity of the mansion. Far from it: pleasure grounds continued to be large and complex. Indeed, in a variety of ways Brown was more than a maker of sweeping parkland, and our concentration on this aspect of his work, important though it is, has arguably distorted our understanding of what, precisely, he provided for his clients. Throughout his career he worked as much as an architect as he did as a landscape designer, not only supplying garden buildings but also making improvements to country houses, or even providing completely new ones. Beginning in the 1750s, but working from 1771 with Henry Holland (his son-in-law from 1773), he provided designs for rebuilding, or extensively modernising, around 20 country houses, including: Lowther in Cumberland (1762), Redgrave in Suffolk (1763), Broadlands (1765) and Cadland in Hampshire (1777), Peper Harow in Sussex (1765), Fisherwick (c.1768), Trentham (c.1773) and Tixall (c.1773) in Staffordshire, Temple Newsam in

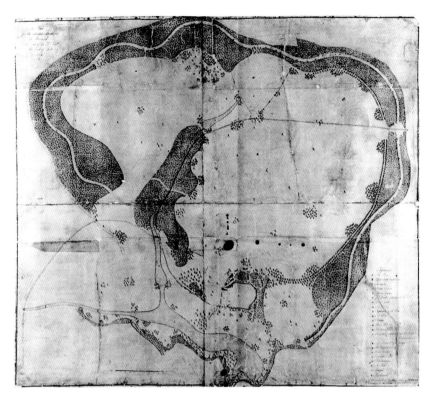

Figure 4.
Bowood, Wiltshire: Brown's plan of 1763 shows well his developed style, with irregular lake, a profusion of drives and rides, and perimeter belt. (By kind permission of the Marquis of Lansdowne and the Bowood Estate)

Yorkshire (1767), Claremont in Surrey (1770), Benham Park in Berkshire (c.1772), Brocklesby in Lincolnshire (1773), Cardiff Castle (1777), Berrington in Herefordshire (1778) and Nuneham Courtenay in Oxfordshire (1780). He also provided clients with new stables, ice houses, land drainage schemes and – as we shall see – kitchen gardens and menageries (places where collections of exotic animals were kept and displayed). In his own words, he was a 'place-maker', supplying his wealthy clients with 'all the elegance and all the comforts that Mankind wants in the Country'.[16]

He did not do all this on his own. The immense sums which came into his bank account from clients soon went out again in the form of large, but intermittent and variable, payments to a range of individuals. These men are often described as his 'foremen' by garden historians but, in reality, were mainly colleagues or sub-contractors, experts in their own particular fields.[17] Many already had, or later

8

developed, successful careers as architects or landscape designers in their own right. Some stayed with Brown for many years: men like Samuel Lapidge, who joined Brown in 1767 and continued his business after his death in 1783; or Jonathan Midgeley, who received payments from Brown from 1760 until 1778.[18] Others, like Nathaniel Richmond or Robert Robinson, only collaborated with him for a few years before going on to make their own reputations as landscape architects, the former mainly in the south-east of England and the latter in Scotland and the north.[19] Some of these men, such as Cornelius Dickinson, come and go from Brown's accounts over the decades, each time being paid relatively small sums and presumably supplying some specialist service or advice – perhaps, in Dickinson's case, relating to the construction of lakes. The scale of Brown's business grew steadily. In 1753, the first year of his account at Drummonds Bank, his recorded receipts totalled £4,924; by 1768 this had risen to £32,279, an enormous sum, equivalent to several million pounds today.[20]

Brown's fully developed landscape style, although owing much to the work of earlier designers like William Kent, differed from theirs in a number of crucial ways. In particular, whereas earlier forms of 'landscape garden' had employed features and buildings to convey messages, ideas and emotions – as most famously at Stowe – in Brown's designs it was the landscape itself, the massing of trees, the disposition of water and the shapes of landforms, that were the message. Earlier forms of irregular landscaping – including Brown's own work – had co-existed with avenues and other geometric features; from the 1760s such elements were only retained in Brown's designs if his clients insisted upon it. And while earlier landscape gardens had worked as a series of set-piece views, Brown's parklands were designed to be experienced as an entirety, through movement along rides and drives, on horseback or in a carriage. Contemporary descriptions leave little doubt that this was a crucial characteristic. Thomas Whately in 1770 thus described the approach to Caversham House in Berkshire, where Brown had landscaped the grounds a few years earlier, almost like a moving film, in a passage that continues, breathlessly, for nearly a thousand words:

> the road passes between the groups [of trees], under a light and lofty arch of ash; and then opens upon a glade, broken on the left only by a single tree; and on the right by several beeches standing so close together as to be but one in appearance; this glade is bounded by a beautiful grove, which in one part spreads a perfect gloom, but in others divides into different clusters, which leave openings for the gleams of light to pour in . . .[21]

Brown himself described his compositions as continuous, textured wholes, like sentences structured by words and punctuation. Hannah More recounted how, in 1782, she:

> Passed two hours in the garden . . . with my friend Mr Brown. I took a very agreeable lecture from him in his art, and he promised to give me taste by inoculation. He illustrates everything he says about gardening by some literary or grammatical allusion. He told me he compared his art to literary composition. "Now *there*", said he, pointing his finger, "I make a comma, and there," pointing to another spot, "where a more decided turn is proper, I make a colon; at another part, where an interruption is desirable to break the view, a parenthesis; now a full stop, and then I begin another subject".[22]

In a similar way, an article in the *Gazetteer and New Daily Advertiser* for 1780 described how the planting of a single willow tree had been Brown's sole contribution to the grounds of the actor David Garrick's villa in Hampton near London, going on to note: 'This single addition Brown compared to punctuation, and not without some felicity of phrase, called it a dot, the presence and operation of which, as it were, made sense of the rest.'[23] The proliferation of rides and drives in Brown's commissions was inextricably linked to this sense of the landscape as a continuous whole, rather than a series of separate and fragmented experiences. It was also related to the smoothness of landforms so favoured by Brown, who would doubtless have approved of Burke's definition of beauty which appeared, significantly, in 1756:

> Most people must have observed the sort of sense they have had, on being swiftly drawn in an easy coach, on a smooth turf, with gradual ascents and declivities. This will give a better idea of the beautiful, and point out its probable cause better than almost anything else.[24]

Yet while it is true that Brown's landscapes worked as a continuum, more than as series of set-piece views, some carefully composed prospects were nevertheless exploited and given prominence in his designs. The few ornamental buildings were positioned in such a way that they formed a focus for a view, but they also acted as vantage points from which the best prospects across the landscape could be enjoyed. Reached by a drive or ride, they often included facilities for making tea and light refreshments. Yet the key 'garden building' was now the mansion itself, which was revealed – teasingly, or suddenly – from the approach drive, and seen to advantage from the other rides and drives running through the park. It was experienced in a manner which differed in important respects from the situation with the older, geometric styles of design. In the words of Thomas Whately,

> An avenue being confined to one termination, and excluding every
> view on the sides, has a tedious sameness throughout; to be great,
> it must be dull: and the object to which it is appropriated, is after
> all seldom shown to advantage . . . buildings, in general, do not
> appear so large, and are not so beautiful, when looked at in front,
> as they are when seen from an angular station, which commands
> two sides at once, and throws them both into perspective.[25]

Brown's fully developed landscapes were simple, elegant, almost minimalist in character. Their essence was the display of the natural landforms, the shape and disposition of which was revealed and accentuated by planting and the use of water: one of the purposes of his lakes was, arguably, to emphasise the shape of the land, the subtlety and complexity of the contours, and contemporary illustrations make clear that their sides were kept scrupulously clear of marginal vegetation (Figure 5). Brown's perimeter belts often followed the line of rising ground, as for example at Chatsworth, the very boundaries of the park thus emerging, as it were, from the natural topography. While contemporaries vaunted their natural character, however, Brown's parks were of course artificial, even engineered, creations. Lakes in particular were alien impositions on the landscape, for outside of a few limited areas – including the Norfolk Broads – very few sizeable bodies of water actually existed in lowland England at the start of Brown's career.

His lakes were unnatural in other respects. Most were made by constructing a dam across a stream or river, and ponding the water back behind it. The dams were often complex pieces of engineering, with tunnels or spillways to allow the lake to be emptied for maintenance and to control water levels.[26] Brown's contracts for Petworth in Sussex in 1756 bound him to 'make a proper plug and Trough to draw down the Water, as likewise a Grate for the discharge of waste water'; that for Bowood in Wiltshire in 1763 noted that there should be 'Plugs, Grates and wastes for the discharge of floods'.[27] Many of Brown's dams had an ornamental cascade on the lower side, as at Charlecote in Oxfordshire. Others, as at Fisherwick in Staffordshire, were disguised as 'sham bridges'. Some, like those of his contemporary designers, had a thick layer of clay on the lake side, covered by a

Figure 5.
Heveningham Hall, Suffolk, as depicted in William Watts' The Seats of the Nobility and Gentry, with carriages running across the smooth turf of Brown's park, and a boat sailing on his lake. (Private collection)

pitching of stones; but sometimes there was a thick central core of clay, especially where the lake had to support the heavy rockwork of a cascade.[28] The sides of the lake could sometimes require the application of layers of rammed clay to make them water-tight, and provision was often made to reduce the rate of silting, as at Bowood, where the arms of the lake had small but separate water bodies at their upper ends, retained by small dams or slip ways, which could act as silt traps. Moreover, while in broad terms the shape of each lake was usually determined by topography, with the retained water simply filling back up the valley behind the dam, nature might need a helping hand. Brown staked out the intended outline on the ground prior to construction but, unless his eye for contours was perfect, his prediction will not always have been correct and some excavation might be required for other reasons – to widen the lake in order to bring it into better view of the mansion, for example.

Other aspects of Brown's designs were equally engineered in character, if effortless and natural in appearance. Large areas of earth were moved, especially to obliterate signs of formal gardens, smooth the slope between house and water, and sometimes to open up distant views or to reduce the gradient on drives. At Chatsworth in Derbyshire, for example, Brown's man, Michael Milliken, worked for four years levelling many of the terraces of the old gardens, filling in the fish ponds and – in particular – grading the sides of the river Derwent, so that it would be visible from the windows of the mansion. Milliken was paid directly by the Duke for 'earth moving', receiving a total of £2,235.[29] But the curious thing is that all this was done with such care and subtlety that, were we not told that such a change had been made, we usually would not guess it. The end result was intended to look 'natural', unconstructed, unaffected by human intervention (Figure 6).

Figure 6.
Chatsworth House, Derbyshire. It took four years' work and £2,235 to level and sculpt the earlier terraces to create a convincing natural look. (Photo: Nadine Hepper, 2016)

Garden historians have long argued about why the style now identified with Lancelot Brown became so popular in the 1760s and 1770s. Some have discussed the issue in simple aesthetic terms, seeing the landscape park as the culmination of the development towards simpler, more 'naturalistic' landscapes, which had begun in the 1720s with Charles Bridgeman and had continued through the 1730s with the work of William Kent and others.[30] Some, following a number of contemporary commentators, have interpreted Brown's landscapes as expressions of eighteenth-century philosophical or political ideas. Many, for example, have argued that the manner in which the informal, serpentine lines of the landscape park combined art and nature reflected the balanced constitution of the nation, which incorporated the principles of both monarchy and democracy.[31] English landscapes thus stood in marked contrast to the gardens of less fortunate nations, especially France, where absolutism was expressed in the serried rows of trees, rigid parterres, and disciplined topiary. There may be much truth in such arguments, but we can usefully add others. In particular, the rise to popularity of the 'landscape' style came at a time of great social and economic change in Britain, and was intimately connected, albeit in complex ways, with a host of wider developments.

Following the political upheavals and civil warfare of the seventeenth century, the eighteenth century was a period of internal peace and stability. Rather than being deeply divided by religion or ideology, as they had been during the Civil War and Commonwealth, the upper strata of society began to coalesce into a single group – often referred to as 'polite society' – which was united around a shared enthusiasm for fashionable consumption and relaxed social encounters. At urban assemblies or at country house gatherings, people of fashion now paid less attention to nuances of social rank, or to the demands of formal etiquette. Instead they interacted on easy, affable terms, carefully avoiding signs of religious or other 'enthusiasm' and keen to display their wit, their appreciation of the latest styles of clothes or furniture, and their knowledge of art and culture.[32] The 'polite' included not only the great landowners and the local gentry but also a new class of financiers, merchants and wealthy businessmen. For this was also a period in which the economy steadily expanded and grew more complex, not least because in the first half of the eighteenth century Britain embarked on its role as a great colonial and trading power. During the period of Brown's career, the pace of economic growth stepped up a gear. From around 1750 the population began to increase rapidly after a period of sluggish demographic growth; the north and west of the country began to industrialise, with rapid expansion in the production of coal and iron and, from the 1770s, in textiles. Added to this the country experienced an 'agricultural revolution' involving the use of new crops and rotations, the adoption of new agricultural techniques like marling and land drainage, the enclosure of the remaining open fields, the reclamation of tracts of common land and the emergence of new regional patterns of agricultural specialisation. Underpinning these great economic changes were major developments in transport infrastructure. Over 300 turnpike acts were passed between 1750 and 1760 alone, affecting some 10,000 miles of road. More important, perhaps, was the growth of the canal network, which began in earnest with the construction of the Bridgewater Canal, connecting the Duke of Bridgewater's coal mines at Worsley with Manchester, between 1759 and 1761 – precisely the same years in which the Duke's grounds at Ashridge in Hertfordshire were being landscaped by Brown and his house rebuilt by Holland.[33] The spirit of 'improvement' was in the air. This word was used by contemporaries to cover a wide range of activities, including the construction of roads and bridges, the reclamation of marginal land, the creation of fashionable town centres for the entertainment of the 'polite', the establishment of plantations – as well as the construction of new mansions and the creation of fashionable landscapes in which to set them.[34] Underlying all these developments was the strong belief – alien to the country in the period before the Civil War of the seventeenth century, but strongly in the ascendant by the first half of the eighteenth – that the present state of things was not God-given and immutable, but provisional, and capable of change. It is easy to see how Brown, with his highly commercialised business dedicated to realising the 'capabilities' of a place, formed part of this wider pattern of vibrant social and economic change.

Indeed, specific aspects of the new style of landscape design clearly reflected and expressed the attitudes of Brown's clients, the character of their world and the sources of their wealth. Most of these people, whether they were established landowners or members of the newly rich, did not derive their income entirely or even primarily from agricultural rents or the produce of their estates. They also prospered from investments, the profits of high office, control over mineral resources and an active involvement in trade, including the trade in slaves. Harewood House in Yorkshire, with its extensive grounds landscaped by Brown, was thus largely funded with income from the Lascelles family's extensive plantations in Barbados, worked by nearly 3,000 slaves.[35] Brown's work at Chatsworth in Derbyshire began in 1759, the year before the lease on the Duke of Devonshire's copper mines at Ecton in Staffordshire was to run out, and just after ore deposits of exceptional quality had been discovered there.[36] Clients like these were a part of a distinctly modern world. Moreover, while the wealthy might live for all or much of their time in the country, their lifestyle and social life was focused on the towns, especially on London and Bath, but also on lesser social centres like Norwich. Their culture was urban rather than rural, and it is in this context in particular that we need to understand Brown's landscape style.

Parks *per se* had thus existed for centuries, but in the form of well-wooded venison farms and hunting grounds. Brown and his contemporaries took this quintessential symbol of gentility and provided it with a fashionable makeover – a polite and elegant veneer – more suited to the age.[37] Deer, the original *raison d'être* of parks, were thus frequently banished in the second half of the eighteenth century and replaced by sheep and cattle, which were less damaging to specimen trees and easier to keep out of shrubberies. While parks might thus survive transformed, their design elevated to an art form, other traditional aspects of the country house landscape, which had once affirmed the owner's direct involvement in the productive life of the countryside, were now banished. Rabbit warrens, farmyards, fish ponds, orchards, nut grounds and vegetable gardens were all removed from the immediate vicinity of the mansion, at the same time as enclosed and geometric gardens were destroyed. Such things seemed inappropriate to an elite now dedicated to fashionable *consumption*, rather than active production, and these features made their homes look too much like the farmhouses of their tenants.

Parks proliferated through the second half of the century, not least because they were cheaper to create and maintain now that they no longer needed to be enclosed with expensive deer-proof fencing. Suitably transformed by the hand of taste, they not only became the principal setting for the great house, but served as insulated and private spaces, surrounded by their woods and plantation belts, at a time when rapid population growth caused escalating rural poverty and increasing social tensions. Park creation almost always involved the closure of footpaths and the diversion of public roads. Not that everyone was excluded from the park. The landscapes of Brown and his contemporaries were designed for the entertainment of the 'polite' – the owner, his family and guests. Lakes were for boating on, rides and drives were for riding and driving along, while belts and clumps served as places to breed and protect pheasants at a time when shooting was becoming more organised and poaching was an increasing problem. Some of the larger parks were open to strangers, either on an informal basis or on specified days; from around 1760 Holkham was open on 'every Tuesday, but no other day. No persons will be admitted that do not tell their names.'[38]

The great houses which lay at the heart of each landscape park likewise developed in ways which made them more suitable for fashionable entertainment. In the early decades of the eighteenth century even the largest country houses usually had only two principal entertaining rooms, the hall and the saloon, the latter lying behind the former and the two together taking up the central part of the building, their presence signalled externally by a pediment or portico. Private apartments ran off from them, suites of rooms arranged as linear sequences of increasing privacy known as *enfilades*.[39] This arrangement of internal space, along linear axes, was mirrored to some extent in the layout of the gardens. The central axis of hall and saloon was thus continued as the central walk in the garden, and beyond, as an avenue through parkland. From the 1730s, however, a few houses – most notably

16

Holkham Hall – began to be provided with more extensive suites of entertaining rooms, which were arranged on a circuit. When the house was used for entertaining, guests could drift easily from one room to the next, alternately taking tea, playing cards, dancing, an arrangement better suited to the new forms of easy, affable social engagement. By the 1750s and 1760s, circuit planning had become the norm.[40]

These changes in domestic planning contributed directly to the new forms of landscape created by Brown and his fellows. As houses organised around linear axes fell from favour, so axial avenues, symmetry and linear vistas became anomalous in their grounds. Instead, the circuit plan of the house was replicated outside, in the disposition of both gardens and park. In the words of the historian Mark Girouard:

> The surroundings of . . . houses were reorganised in much the same way as the interiors, and for similar reasons. . . . Guests or visitors, having done the circuit of the rooms, did the circuit of the grounds. Just as, at a big assembly, tea was served in one room and cards laid out in another, the exterior circuit could be varied by stopping at a temple to take tea, or at a rotunda to scan the view through a telescope.[41]

The proliferation of rides and drives facilitated the use of the park in these kinds of ways, especially on the part of women. Earlier deer parks had essentially been areas for male rather than female recreation. Hunting deer, while never exclusively an activity undertaken by men, was predominantly associated with them.[42] So, too, was the practice of fast riding across the open parkland, for although upper-class women did regularly ride, modesty and mode of dress tended to ensure that this was in a manner – usually side saddle (with both legs on the same side of the horse) – which reduced the speed with which they could move, and made it difficult to negotiate the rough parkland turf. In the middle decades of the century improvements to riding dress, especially the shortening of the skirt and riding coat, and a more masculine cut, made riding easier for women, but these innovations were widely criticised. The gravel drives, turf rides and smooth contours of Brown's parks ensured that they could be enjoyed in equal measure by both sexes, in carriages or on horseback.

The rise of the landscape style was thus related in part to developments in country house architecture: and there were other links between the design of houses, and that of their grounds. Brown's earlier landscapes had accompanied a house built in Palladian style, the refined form of classicism which became fashionable from the late 1710s, and which was based on the work of Inigo Jones (an architect from the previous century) and, in particular, on the designs of the sixteenth-century Italian Andreas Palladio.[43] The latter, in turn, had modelled his buildings on what was then known about the architecture of classical antiquity, which in truth was not a great deal. Palladio's designs for country houses were thus based, not on the *houses* of the ancients, but on their temples. As the antiquarian Allan Ramsay observed in 1762:

> The present taste in architecture was formed, not upon the palaces and dwelling-houses of the ancient Greeks and Romans, of which there were no vestiges at the revival of the arts, but upon their temples and other buildings, from which the ornamental part has been borrowed and applied to domestic use, in a manner abundantly absurd, for the most part . . . which, nevertheless, custom has rendered agreeable to the sight.[44]

His comments reflect the fact that in the middle decades of the eighteenth century a more accurate knowledge of classical art and architecture began to be disseminated across western Europe, as a result of excavations at places like Herculaneum and Pompeii, and as a consequence of archaeological expeditions to Greece.[45] Architects like Nicholas Revett and, in particular, Robert Adam were swept along with this new enthusiasm for classical civilisation. They began to design country houses and other buildings which were not merely based on Greek and Roman precedents but were informed by a more general taste for simplicity in form and outline which was derived from it.[46] More importantly, 'Neoclassicism' also embraced aspects of interior design. It became apparent, from excavations at Herculaneum especially, that Roman houses had been decorated with light, rather delicate painted schemes, featuring figures, foliage, birds and much else, and these Adam and others took as their inspiration for the remodelling of domestic interiors in England.[47] Soon Neoclassical taste was also influencing the objects placed within these spaces, from the pottery produced by Josiah Wedgwood, decorated with figures in classical dress, florets, urns and the like, to the elegant furniture of Thomas Chippendale.[48] All these things became fashionable from the early 1760s, just as Brown's fully developed style was emerging. Brown and his business could hardly be immune from this significant shift in taste. His early houses were in the Palladian mode, but by the late 1760s, at Claremont, he and Henry Holland were producing designs which were more Neoclassical than Palladian in inspiration, and

Figure 7.
Benham Park near Newbury, Berkshire, viewed from the south. Built in the late 1770s, this Neoclassical composition by Brown and his son-in-law, Henry Holland, appears perfectly in harmony with its landscape of minimalist simplicity. The upper floor is a nineteenth-century addition. (Photo: Tom Williamson)

by the 1770s places like Benham Park in Berkshire or Berrington in Herefordshire were entirely Neoclassical in style. Many of Brown's landscapes were created at the same time as houses were being remodelled by Robert Adam or other Neoclassical architects. The increasing simplicity, almost minimalism, of Brown's compositions echoed the principles of the new architecture, with their emphasis on planes and on distinct, continuous outlines. A landscape designed by Brown made a perfect setting for a Neoclassical house (Figure 7). Brown's designs also mirrored the ideas and concepts underlying the new architecture, the emphasis of Adam and others on the simple and the 'pure', their rejection of 'superfluous ornament' and above all their belief that architectural forms were to be derived from nature's beauties, distilled through observation and abstraction. To Brown, creating landscapes was not a matter of ephemeral fashion or whim, but of systematic observation and the application of appropriate enhancements.

> Place-making, and a good English Garden, depend entirely upon
> Principle and have very little to do with Fashion, for it is a word
> that in my opinion disgraces Science wherever it is found.[49]

Yet Neoclassicism was not simply a matter of harking back to antiquity. Indeed, the styles of Greece and Rome, in this age of science and industry, were to be improved upon, not just slavishly copied.[50] Right across Europe the new taste was closely allied with the spirit of the Enlightenment, and in England too it was broadly aligned with the spirit of improvement, with modernisation.[51] And this, perhaps, is the last point we need to emphasise about Brown's landscapes: the way in which they both reflected and represented other, more practical aspects of 'improvement', other forms of modernity. Two examples make this point well. We noted earlier the crucial importance in England's economic expansion of the new canal network, but 'navigations' were only one aspect of a wider interest in water management in the eighteenth century. Not only were the first factories powered by water power, rather than by steam – necessitating the construction of mill ponds and often very complex systems of supply channels – the control of water was also of vital importance in the improvement of agriculture. The eighteenth century saw the spread across southern and western Britain of new techniques of water-meadow irrigation, while elsewhere – especially in the east – new methods of systematic field drainage, using simple bush drains, were widely adopted in the period of Brown's career.[52] There were, moreover, new concerns about the effects of damp conditions on human health on the part of the social elite – a desire to escape the deleterious effects of 'miasmas' – so that some houses were rebuilt on new, more elevated sites, leaving behind the moats and fish ponds which had formerly been indispensable adjuncts to a mansion.[53] Brown's lakes, and his complex land drainage schemes – aimed at creating a dry setting for the house, but distant views of controlled, engineered water – should be read as part of this wider interest in water and its management. Indeed, on occasions lake-making was a way of dealing with areas of damp, marshy ground which could not be effectively drained. Lord Dacre described in 1759 how Brown's proposed lake within the park at Belhus in Essex would be:

> A very great ornament to that side of the Park and quite change the
> Face of it. By what I have said you will immediately conceive that
> all the rushy part of Bumstead Mead will be converted into water,
> and that the Black moory soil will be taken away till we come to
> the parts of the meadow that rise and where the soil is gravel.[54]

The improvement of the nation's roads, through turnpike trusts and a variety of innovations in construction, was another key precondition for economic expansion, and this likewise had connections with Brown's landscapes. The rapid increase in road traffic resulting from the creation of turnpikes led to popular demand for shorter routes, and thus to a marked upsurge in bridge construction.[55] Bridges were a pleasing and topical novelty, and it is no coincidence that they feature in so many of Brown's parks, with the approach drive often brought, usually gratuitously, across a river (as at Burghley or Chatsworth), a narrow lake (as at Shortgrove in Essex) or one arm of a larger lake (as at Bowood). Alongside the improvements of roads, there were significant developments in the design of carriages. The better opportunities for travel saw a range of technical innovations, especially in better forms of suspension. They also witnessed the development, through the 1750s and 1760s, of new types of small, light pleasure vehicle: the landau – a four-wheeled carriage with a two-part hood that could be thrown back so that passengers might enjoy the open air; the curricle – a light two-wheeled carriage; and the phaeton – a light open-topped vehicle on which the seats were raised high above the ground, and which was known for its ability to negotiate sharp bends, the sports car of its age.[56] Now that major roads were less likely to be pitted with potholes, driving could be an enjoyable leisure activity. The networks of drives and rides in Brown's parks represented a private extension of the improved road network, and reflected new possibilities of, and a new attitude towards, travel in horse-drawn vehicles, as well as the new forms of such vehicles which were now available. If these improvements in transport had not occurred, it is hard to believe that Brown's serpentine drives – and the way in which his landscapes were designed around them – would have become so popular with his clients.

By the time of Brown's death in 1783, landscape parks – in a variety of forms and of various sizes – could be found throughout Britain, although only a minority were actually designed by Brown himself. Norfolk could boast perhaps as many as a hundred examples: although the county lay remote from fashionable London, it was no economic or cultural backwater. Some of the most important families amongst the Whigs – the dominant political group for most of the eighteenth century – lived here, including the Walpoles, the Townshends and the Cokes. Norwich was still, in 1750, the third largest city in England, after London and Bristol. The county's textile industry was, with each passing decade, increasingly challenged by the new factories located in north and west England, where undulating terrain made it easier to harness water power. However, Norfolk was by now embarking on its new career, as England's premier farming county, the very heart of the agricultural revolution and the home of 'Turnip' Townshend and

'Coke of Norfolk'. Enclosure, reclamation and the adoption of new methods ensured that farm output increased and agricultural rents rose steadily, providing landowners with the income required to make fashionable improvements to their house and grounds.

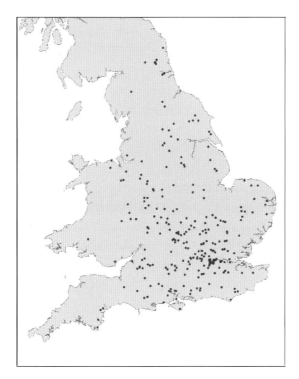

Figure 8.
A map of Brown's commissions, showing both 'possible' and 'certain' sites. Note the strong concentration of sites in the area around London, and the thinner scatter through the west Midlands. (Courtesy of Jon Gregory and Sarah Spooner, University of East Anglia)

Capability Brown only designed three major landscapes in Norfolk – at Kimberley, Langley and Melton Constable – although he had a hand in a fourth, Holkham, and his involvement has been suggested at a number of other places. Three sites is not a very large total, especially compared to the number of commissions which Brown undertook in counties nearer London or in parts of the Midlands (Figure 8). But as we will demonstrate, carefully studied – using a combination of archive research and recording in the field – these places can throw important new light on Brown's activities and style more generally.

CHAPTER 2　　　　　　　KIMBERLEY

Kimberley Hall and Park. (Photo: ©Mike Page Aerial Photography)

Introduction

Kimberley Park is situated in south Norfolk around 3 miles (c.5 kilometres) north-west of Wymondham and 8 miles (c.13 kilometres) south-west of Norwich. It lies to the south of the Yare Valley in an area of farmland and woodland on clay soils with some gravel overlying chalk. The river Tiffey, a tributary of the Yare, runs from south to north through the park and the present hall stands on a high point, where the land slopes gently down to the south-west, towards a lake. The village of Kimberley lies to the west of the park where the parish church of St Peter stands beside the former village school, built in 1850 by the Hon. Mrs Wodehouse.[57] On Wymondham Road, Attleborough Lodge (one of the former lodges to the estate) is a picturesque, thatched building in cottage orné style. At the north-east entrance to the park, on the Barnham Broom Road, are a pair of early nineteenth-century, one-storey square lodges, marking the present entrance to Kimberley. The church has its origins in the twelfth century, but much of the building is later, including the sixteenth-century tower with the upper part rebuilt in 1631, with further restorations in the nineteenth and early twentieth centuries.

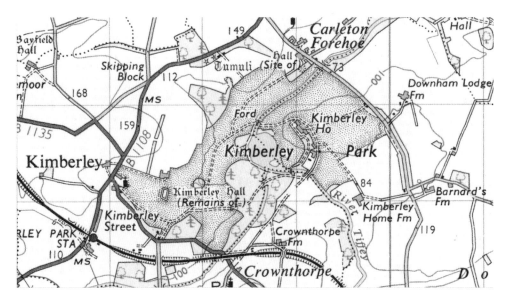

Figure 9.
Location of Kimberley Park. (Reproduced from 1954 Ordnance Survey 1-inch map with the kind permission of the Ordnance Survey)

For many centuries Kimberley was home to the Wodehouse family and the development of the hall and its landscape reflect their growing importance as they rose to become, by the eighteenth century, one of the leading families in the county. The area has a long history of settlement, and archaeological evidence of the various houses that existed at Kimberley over several centuries still remains. The park is a fine example of a Capability Brown landscape but his work is only part of the complex history of the manors and parks of Kimberley and Downham, which has involved many other designers and architects.

Kimberley before Brown

The Wodehouse family held high office across the centuries, as Sheriffs of both London and Norfolk and as Recorders. They have been close to monarchs, travelled with kings in foreign and domestic wars, and held positions of authority by royal appointment. Younger sons served as chaplains, as stewards to religious orders, or served in the Navy, often maintaining important links with other noble and influential individuals. Francis Blomefield, in his *Essay towards a Topographical History of Norfolk*, suggests that the Wodehouse family can be traced back to Sir Constantine de Wodehouse, knighted by Henry I,[58] although it has been suggested that the family's early pedigree and Norfolk connections were exaggerated.[59] Nevertheless, Blomefield quotes seventeenth-century writer and

Figure 10.
Kimberley Hall from the park, looking towards the north-west corner of the house. (Photo: Roger Last, 2007)

illustrator, Henry Peacham, as declaring them to be 'gentlemen of good rank, in and before the time of King John'.[60] The family came to Kimberley as a result of the marriage of Sir John Wodehouse to Margaret, daughter and sole heiress of Sir Thomas Fastolf. This was the first and one of the most significant of a series of advantageous marriages that were to bring the family wealth and property over the next few centuries. On the death of Sir Thomas in 1384 Sir John gained the estates at Kimberley, although disputes over Margaret's inheritance continued for many years.[61] Henry IV knighted Sir John and his son, John Wodehouse, Esq., served as Gentleman of the Privy Chamber to Henry IV and later as Esquire of the Body to Henry V. It was this John who fought at Agincourt with such distinction that the family became known as the 'Agincourt Wodehouses',[62] and the king bestowed upon the family a new crest featuring a hand issuing out of clouds, holding a club and the motto 'Frappé fort' or 'Strike strong' with *Agincourt* beneath the arms. The ancient family crest of a wild man or savage was omitted, but instead two such figures were placed as supporters to the arms[63] (Figure 11).

The property acquired by Sir John was focused on a manor house which stood within a moated site south of the present park, in what is now known as Falstoff's Wood, but Sir John decided to build a new house on a second moated site some 900 metres (just over half a mile) to the west, within what was probably an existing deer park. The house was completed early in the fifteenth century but it is likely that there were further periods of building through the fifteenth and sixteenth centuries. The moat and low brick walls remain, the latter including some sixteenth-century brickwork.[64] Also during the sixteenth century, sometime before 1540, elaborate pleasure grounds and water gardens were laid out to the east of the hall, overlooking the Old Park, either by Sir Thomas Wodehouse or by his son, Sir Roger (d. 1588).[65]

Figure 11.
Crest of the Wodehouse family. (Norfolk Record Office. HMN 7/296.773X1)

Some of the later work to the house may have been carried out in connection with the visit of Elizabeth I in 1578 on her progress from Norwich to Cambridge.[66] It was at this time that Sir Roger received his knighthood, which was bestowed by the queen at Sir Edward Clare's house at Blickling near Aylsham. Probably preparations for the visit were not solely confined to the house but included the landscape around too. Pleasure gardens were already in existence by the 1570s but Patsy Dallas has suggested that other parts of the grounds were developed in anticipation of the queen's visit: *The Newe Lawne Closes* north of the hall were enclosed in the park in the 1570s and beside them, just off the Norwich Road, is an area described as The Queen's Corner on a survey of 1700 by Samuel Gilpin. Adjacent to this, a large U-shaped earthwork survived well into the twentieth century (it is visible on 1946 RAF aerial photographs, but has since been removed and its site levelled), which may have been the location for a welcoming ceremony. Such events were common when the queen arrived at a country house and included speeches, pageants and plays.[67] Inside the hall preparations included the provision of a lavish throne for the queen, described as 'of crimson velvet, richly embroidered with gold, having on it the arms of Wodehouse, with the supporters,

&c., all in curious work'.[68]   The throne is now in the Burrell Collection in Glasgow.

The Wodehouse family continued to live in the house built by Sir John, which was also known as Wodehouse Tower, until the middle of the seventeenth century. In 1649 Sir Philip Wodehouse, son of Sir Thomas, acquired Downham Manor, to the east of the Kimberley estate, from Richard Buxton, and subsequently moved there. A year after the death of Sir Thomas in 1658, Sir Philip demolished Wodehouse Tower, part of which had fallen into disrepair, and its fate is lamented in a poem supposedly written by Sir Philip, and quoted by Blomefield:

> First fell Queen Elizabeth's brave lodging roome,
> Then the fair stately hall, to ruin came,
> Next falls the vast great chamber arch'd on high,
> With golden pendents fretted sumptuously,
> Yet of four parts, three still remained the seat,
> Unto that heir, who first was baronet,
> And to his son, 'till the long parliament,
> Nobles and gentry, sunk to discontent,
> In which sad humour he lets all the rest,
> Of this fair fabrick sink into its dust,
> Down falls the chapel, last the goodly towre,
> Tho' of materials so firm and stowre,
> Time scarce uncements them, like dismal fate,
> Does England suffer both in church and state,
> But these may God re-build and raise again,
> By restauration of our Sovereign.[69]

Sir Philip died in 1681 and was succeeded by his grandson, Sir John Wodehouse (1669–1754), his eldest son, Sir Thomas, having died of smallpox in 1671. Sir John was just twelve years old when he inherited and it was not until the early 1700s that he began to make plans to build a new mansion, which he proposed erecting on yet another site within the old deer park, around 500 metres (a third of a mile) north of the site of Wodehouse Tower.

The first indication we have of Sir John's plans is the survey of the Kimberley estate, made by Samuel Gilpin in 1700, overlaid with the outline of a new house. The building shown has a central range flanked at each end by projecting bays, enclosing large square courtyards, and is marked 'New House Desin'd to be Built' (Figure 12). Although there is no conclusive evidence, this design was probably by William Talman (1650–1719). Talman was a leading country house architect of the day; his work included the design of the south and east ranges of Chatsworth and he was Comptroller of Works to William III from 1689 to 1702.[70] Talman was certainly working for Sir John by early 1701 when a payment of £58 15s. was made to him from Sir John's account at Hoare's Bank, although exactly what this was for is not specified. [71]

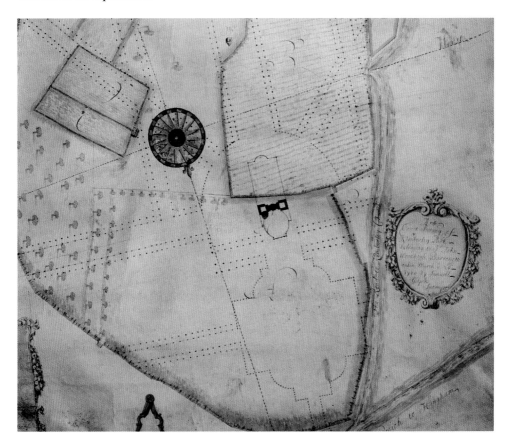

Figure 12.
Detail of a survey of Kimberley Park by Samuel Gilpin dated 20 March 1700. The survey is overlaid with a plan for the layout of formal gardens and 'New House desin'd to be Built'. (Private Collection. Photo: Roger Last, 2015)

Gilpin's plan also shows a proposed formal garden layout in grand style with avenues stretching out into the surrounding park. John Harris has suggested that this design was by landscape gardener George London, who worked closely with Talman on a number of houses. If that were the case, it adds weight to the argument that Talman drew up the first plan for the house, as it is likely he would have involved London in designing the gardens. [72]

Sometime after 1700 Talman prepared a design for a new house, different in style to that shown on Gilpin's survey. This was for a two-and-a-half storey hall with a central block of seven bays and square towers at each corner of the building

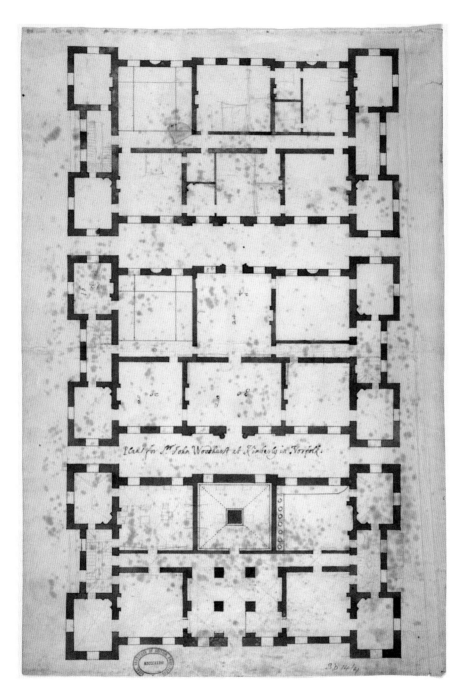

Plan for Mr John Woodhouse at Kimberly in Norfolk.

Figure 13.
Design for Kimberley Hall by William Talman. The drawing is undated but must be after Gilpin's survey of 1700 (which shows a different outline for the hall) and before building work started around 1712. The plan shows the layout of each storey of the building, the ground floor at the bottom of the image. (Courtesy of RIBA Collections)

29

(Figure 13). It was built, not in the old deer park, but to the east of the river Tiffey, in Downham, and is the house we see today, although much modified in the middle decades of the eighteenth century. No drawing of the elevation exists, only the plan, and the images we have of the Hall all post-date the alterations made in the 1750s, so we cannot be certain of its appearance when first built. However, it was likely to have been a large, plain Baroque mansion, with a rather austere appearance, probably similar to designs by Talman for Fetcham Park in Surrey for Arthur Moore c.1705 and Panton Hall in Lincolnshire for Joseph Gace c.1719.[73]

The hall as we see it today is very much as it was in the mid-eighteenth century, built in fine red bricks with nine bays, the central three projecting slightly and surmounted by a pediment, and with square pavilion towers at each corner. Two detached one-and-a-half storey wings provided accommodation for offices and services and later, in the 1830s, were linked to the main house as part of a further scheme of alterations (Figure 14).

Figure 14.
Kimberley Hall, south-west front, from an early twentieth-century postcard. (Private Collection)

Building began in 1712 and a map of 1714, surveyed by James Anderton, shows the house and wings in elevation. Interestingly, it appears to lack the corner towers shown on Talman's design, and which are such a prominent feature of the building today. It is possible that they were not added until the next phase of building work, which took place in the 1750s under Sir John's successor, Sir Armine Wodehouse. In front of the house to the south-west a rectangular courtyard is shown and a large area of about 5 hectares (12 acres) marked 'The Gardens and Orchard', sloping down towards the river Tiffey. However, the plan gives no indication of how these gardens were laid out (Figure 15).

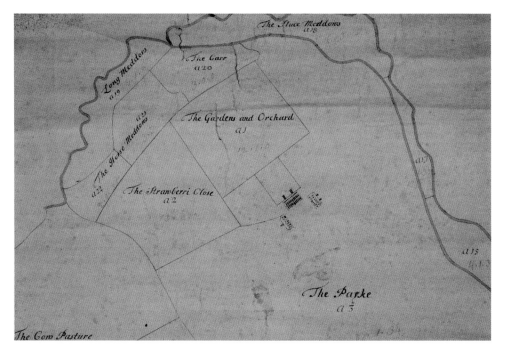

Figure 15.
Detail of a map of Kimberley Hall and grounds surveyed by James Anderton, 1714. Sir John Wodehouse's new house is shown in elevation.
(Private Collection. Photo: Roger Last, 2015)

The next plan of the site that exists was surveyed c.1755 by Thomas Nollorth and shows the changes which had taken place to the park and surrounding landscape by the time that Sir Armine inherited in 1754 (Figure 16). The gardens and orchard have been swept away to be replaced by more informal tree planting and there is now a lake, with two straight sides and two irregular ones. These changes are likely to have been made sometime in the 1730s or 1740s in an attempt to introduce some informality in keeping with the fashion of the time.

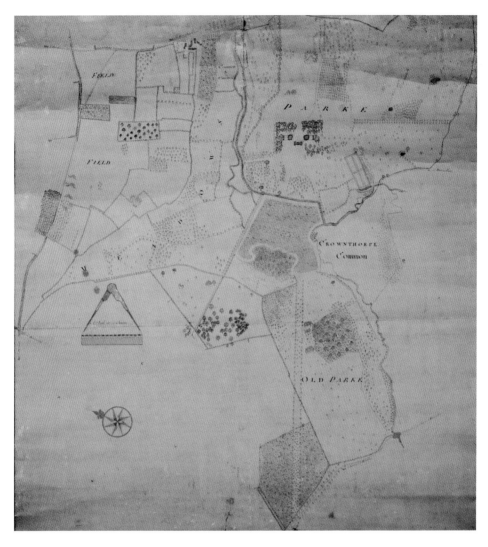

Figure 16.
Plan by Thomas Nollorth c.1755 showing Kimberley after Prowse's work to the house and
before Capability Brown was commissioned to work on the landscape.
(Private Collection. Photo: Roger Last, 2015)

Blomefield describes the lake and river in the entry for Wymondham:

> The house stands on the summit of a hill, in a most pleasant park,
> and commands two fine views, the western one overlooks a valley
> with a rivulet in the midst, a large basin of water of about 12 or 14
> acres, rendering it most delightful that way, as the fine *visto* doth
> on the other side, which commands the valley, and terminates in a
> most agreeable landscape towards Barford.[74]

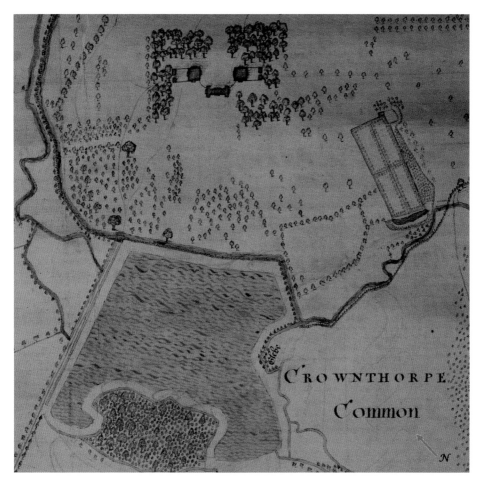

Figure 17.
Detail of Nollorth's plan depicting the lake prior to Brown's work, with its semi-formal outline, and around the hall formal blocks of trees are shown. The kitchen garden is now in place to the south-east of the hall.

Later in the volume, describing Kimberley, he adds:

> The piece of water which lies in this parish, and is there said to contain about 12 or 14 acres, is now extended into a noble *lake* of about 28 acres, which seems to environ a large wood or carr on its west side; rendering its appearance to the house much more grand and delightful; the rivulet that ran on its east side is now made a *serpentine river*, laid out in a neat manner, and is the boundary to the park, on the west and north sides, being above a mile in length.[75]

33

So the lake was already in existence before Brown first came to Kimberley, although he was to introduce significant changes to its outline, and to that of the river Tiffey itself, in his two plans for the site. Also appearing on Nollorth's plan is a kitchen garden, some 200 metres (220 yards) south-east of the hall, and so this clearly pre-dates Brown's involvement.

Figure 18.
Sir Armine Wodehouse, Colonel of the East Norfolk Militia, at a review of the Regiment, just outside Norwich, in 1759. The castle and cathedral can be seen in the background on the left of the painting. Attributed to David Morier. (Courtesy of the Council of the National Army Museum, London)

Sir Armine Wodehouse's alterations

Sir Armine Wodehouse succeeded to the baronetcy and estate on the death of Sir John in 1754. The Wodehouses were the leading Tory family in Norfolk from the sixteenth to the eighteenth centuries and Sir Armine had been elected to Parliament for Norfolk in 1737, a seat he was to hold until 1768. His politics were described as 'authoritarian Toryism, strongly coloured by family tradition and old rankling resentments'.[76] He lacked preferment and advancement in government, which may have contributed to his attitude. When defeated in the 1768 election he wrote to Lord Townshend that he had 'not the least inclination to serve my country' and that he intended to spend the 'remainder of my life as a country gentleman . . . employ myself in my own affairs and as an overseer and surveyor'.[77] He was, however, active as a colonel in the East Norfolk Militia, in which capacity he was painted, in full uniform, at a review of the Regiment in 1759 (Figure 18).

Sir Armine had made a good marriage, to Letitia, eldest daughter and co-heir of Sir Edmund Bacon of Garboldisham, Norfolk and Redgrave, Suffolk. The Bacons had acquired substantial funds through the marriage of Sir Nicholas Bacon to a wealthy ward of the Bures family in the sixteenth century, as well as from the income from a number of stewardships. At the time of his death Sir Nicholas was one of the richest landowners in Suffolk.

Sir Armine Woodhouse was forty years old when he inherited Kimberley and almost immediately embarked on 'very great additions and improvements'.[78] The changes to the house were made under the direction of Thomas Prowse (c.1708–1767), a 'gentleman architect' who designed buildings essentially as a hobby, mainly for friends (Figure 19). Prowse was born in Somerset and served as MP for the county between 1740 and 1767 so Sir Armine would probably have first met him through his Parliamentary work. Later there was to be a family connection between the two men when Prowse's daughter, Elizabeth, married Sir John Mordaunt, 7th Baronet, the son of Sir Charles Mordaunt and Sophia Wodehouse, Sir Armine's sister.

Amateur architects were a common feature of the seventeenth and eighteenth centuries, often working with professional architects, who would draw up plans and supervise work. At Kimberley, Thomas Prowse engaged John Sanderson (d. 1774) to act as executive architect. Sanderson mainly worked in the Palladian style and was also a skilled designer of rococo decoration. He had collaborated with Prowse at Hatch Court in Somerset and Copped Hall in Essex, and both men had also worked with another famous amateur, Sanderson Miller, at Hagley Hall in Warwickshire. As well as acting as executive architect for the alterations, Sanderson designed some of the interiors at Kimberley, continuing to work there as late as 1770, and the later phases of his work increasingly reflected the new

Neoclassical taste.[79] Interestingly, he also designed the rococo interiors at Langley Park in the 1750s.[80]

The alterations at Kimberley were extensive and estate records for the period are remarkably detailed with accounts showing payments to bricklayers, masons and plasterers as well as for deliveries of materials including stone, slate and timber. These detailed records shed much light on the process of building during this period.[81] Unfortunately no plan of the proposed changes has survived so their character remains unclear, but from the records and letters between Prowse and Sir Armine it is possible to gauge the type and scale of the work done.

Figure 19.
Thomas Prowse, a portrait by Thomas Gainsborough, early 1760s. (Private Collection)

Inside the house the layout was opened up, with mention of 'throwing rooms together', and removing a wall to enlarge the Great Parlour, a load-bearing beam being installed in its place. Other work was carried out to Sir Armine's library and only a few of the rooms seem to have escaped work by plasterers and carpenters. Extensive alterations were also made to the kitchens and offices.

Externally, changes were made to the windows to make them a uniform size, altering those spanning 3 foot 6 inches in width to 4 feet (a lot of work for a six-inch gain!). Prowse mentions 'bring[ing] your windows opposite each other'.[82] This would have given the house a much more symmetrical and harmonious look. Other external changes included removing a parapet wall and – probably, but not certainly – the addition of the four corner turrets. There is conflicting evidence as to whether these were added by Prowse, or extensively remodelled, as part of the improvements. The elevation of the hall which forms a detail in James Anderton's 1714 survey does not show the towers and John Neale described in 1820 how the 'additions' made by Sir Armine included the provision of 'four rooms at each angle of the building'.[83] The scale of work carried out by the bricklayers indicated by the building records, and the fact that the exterior brickwork of the turrets does not align exactly with that of the main house, also suggests that they were constructed at this time. We should note as well the striking similarity of the turrets to those at Hagley Hall (built 1754–60) where Prowse worked with Sanderson Miller, and that this house in turn was influenced by Holkham Hall. Perhaps Sir Armine wanted to emulate his Norfolk neighbour? Closer to Kimberley, he could also have been inspired by the changes to Langley Park in the early 1750s, which updated a Baroque house with a more fashionable Palladian appearance, partly by adding corner turrets.

The building records for this work are headed 'An Account of the Charges in taking down the Old House and Building the Turrets &c. begun 24th March 1755'.[84] This could be interpreted as referring to taking down the corners of the house in order to build in the corner towers to the main structure. A. M. F. Pickard has suggested that the towers were part of the original design, but that the crowning turrets were added as part of the later works, although also noting that much time was spent in matching the new work at all levels which seems to discount this possibility.[85] On balance the evidence seems to point to the towers being added during the 1750s but questions remain and we cannot be absolutely certain of their date. It is clear, however, that the design of the turrets as we see them today was part of Prowse's work at Kimberley.

With his house now updated, with a more fashionable Palladian look, Sir Armine turned his attentions to the landscape around the house, and commissioned Lancelot 'Capability' Brown to redesign the park.

Brown's work at Kimberley

Brown's work at Kimberley spans a period of over 15 years, from 1762 to at least 1778, and he thus remodelled the landscape for two generations of the Wodehouse family: Sir Armine Wodehouse, 5th Baronet and his son John, 6th Baronet and 1st Baron Wodehouse of Kimberley. Brown drew up two plans for the site, both of which still exist. Brown's accounts at Coutts Bank show payments made in 1763–6, 1771, 1773, and 1777–8 for the work done, amounting in total to £2,900.[86] He charged for three further journeys in 1782.

Shortly after Brown's first visits to Kimberley he was also carrying out work for the Astleys at Melton Constable and the Beauchamp-Proctors at Langley Park, both families with whom the Wodehouses had close connections, politically, socially and by marriage. Blanch, daughter of Sir Philip Wodehouse, married Sir Jacob Astley in 1661 and later, in 1815, Sir Armine's son, the Revd Philip Wodehouse, married Amelia Beauchamp-Proctor.

Brown's first plan, in 1762, involved extending the park, creating a more informal landscape, adding new gravel paths and rides, and making major changes to the lake and surrounding area (Figures 20 and 21).

The area of the old medieval deer park, to the west of the river Tiffey, together with adjoining areas of meadow and woodland, were now to be brought within the park; so too was land lying to the north-west, stretching as far as the road from Watton to Norwich. The new boundary of the park is shown planted with a narrow wooded belt and clumps of trees were to be created on the four bronze age 'howes' or barrows beside the Watton Road. South of the lake the avenue of trees in the Old Park, shown on Nollorth's plan, was to be removed and the planting in this area significantly thinned.

However, the major changes that Brown proposed were to the lake and river. Although the lake looks like a very 'Brownian' feature, it was already in existence by the time he started work at Kimberley. Fortuitously, it was in exactly the spot, in view of the house across the lawn, that he would mostly likely have chosen for an entirely new water feature. But in the early 1760s it was still halfway between 'formal' and 'informal' in layout, with two ruler-straight sides. His plan was to give it a much more natural look, making the sides more irregular and redirecting and widening sections of the river Tiffey. The narrow meanders of the existing river are shown with faint dotted lines on the plan. The Tiffey's course was to run behind (to the west of) a wooded promontory which extended into the lake, with two 'embayments' on either side. Brown also planned to create two small islands.

38

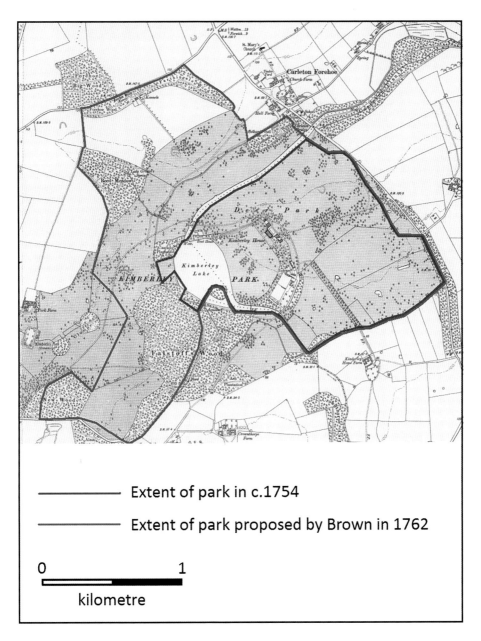

Extent of park in c.1754

Extent of park proposed by Brown in 1762

0   1

kilometre

Figure 20.
The extent of Kimberley gardens and park as proposed by Brown in his 1762 plan and prior to his work at the site overlaid on the Ordnance Survey First Edition 6-inch map. The red line shows the park and gardens in the mid-1750s and the blue line the area of expansion envisaged by Brown. (Map reproduced from 1887 Ordnance Survey with the kind permission of the Ordnance Survey)

Figure 21.
'A Plan of the Intended Alterations at Kimberley in Norfolk'. Brown's first plan of 1762.
(Private Collection)

To the south, the river was to be widened into something described as the 'Intended Water', with a small feed into the lake passing beneath a wooden bridge. From the western embayment the water flows out of the lake via a cascade or dam. Below the cascade the straightened and widened river Tiffey formed a feature often described as a 'long water' in the eighteenth century.

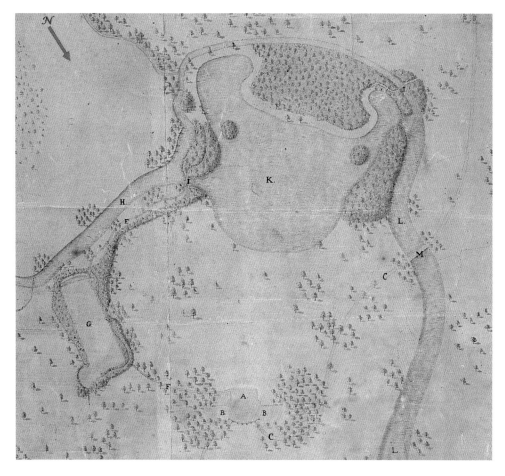

Figure 22.
Detail of the design for the lake from Brown's plan of 1762. (As Figure 14)

KEY FOR BROWN'S 1762 PLAN

A	The House	I	Wooden Bridges
B	The Offices	K	The Old Water
C	The West Approach to the House	L	An Intended River
F	Intended Gravel Path	M	A Stone Bridge
G	Kitchen Garden		
H	Intended Water		

The lake formed a key part of a network of walks around the park, and the plan shows a new winding gravel path running from the house, passing the kitchen garden before crossing onto one of the embayments via the wooden bridge mentioned above and continuing as a walk around the lake. Another footbridge led off on the north-west side of the lake, allowing visitors to walk into the wider landscape beyond.

In the park to the west of the house a proposed 'Dairy and Tea Room' is marked on the plan. These were popular features in the eighteenth century and were introduced by Brown at a number of other sites such as Castle Ashby in Northamptonshire, but there is no evidence that the example proposed for Kimberley was ever built.

The main entrance to Kimberley prior to Brown's work had been from the north-east but Brown proposed a new, additional approach to the house from the south-west, with a lodge at the entrance, and which crossed the widened river Tiffey via a new stone bridge placed just downstream of the cascade. The plan also includes a number of drives around the outer park, which would have allowed carriages to traverse the perimeter.

Although some of the changes proposed by Brown in 1762 were carried out, the scheme was by no means fully realised; exactly how much was implemented is unclear. Two surveys exist of the park, both by S. King, surveyor, which were made just before Brown returned to prepare his second scheme in 1778. The first is entitled 'Survey of Sr A. Wodehouse's Lake with Crownthorpe Common &c.', (dated 1777); and the second, 'A Plan of the Lake, Plantations &c. belonging to Sr John Wodehouse' dated 1778 (Figure 23). Both show that changes had been made to the outline of the lake, although not as planned by Brown in 1762. The northern and western edges are still shown as being relatively straight, the wooded indent on the south-western side has been removed and the outline simplified. Two islands have been added, a larger one to the south and a small one to the east. King's 1778 plan, which covers a greater area, shows that a gravel path had been created along the side of the kitchen garden and crossing the river by a footbridge, although rather than running around the edge of the lake it skirted its shore for a short distance before continuing south into 'The Olde Parke' beyond. The same survey also shows that much planting and thinning of trees had taken place in the area between the hall and the lake, and here Brown's plans do appear to have been carried out. In particular, the block of trees to the north-west of the house shown on Nollorth's plan of c.1755 has been largely removed (King's map does not show the area to the north-east of the house, but probably the geometric blocks of trees on this side were also removed at this time as part of Brown's scheme).

The pattern of trees on the lawn sloping down to the lake has also been made more natural and a group of conifers is shown which are likely to have been planted by

Brown. Botanist and dendrophile James Grigor visited Kimberley around 1841 when writing his *Eastern Arboretum*, and described the trees to be found on the lawn, particularly singling out for comment 'two clumps of lofty Scotch pines standing in the foreground, which in such a site are invaluable'. [87] Given their size and likely age these must surely have been planted by Brown when he was working at Kimberley some 60 or 70 years earlier. A drawing by Humphry Repton of around 1780 shows the park just after Brown had completed his work at the site and includes a group of conifers to the right of the hall, enclosed by a fence (Figure 24). These could possibly be those described later by Grigor. Repton has added a group of figures engaged in fishing in the lake, an illustration of how the landscape park could provide activities and entertainment for its owners. The drawing is also significant as it is the earliest known view of the house.

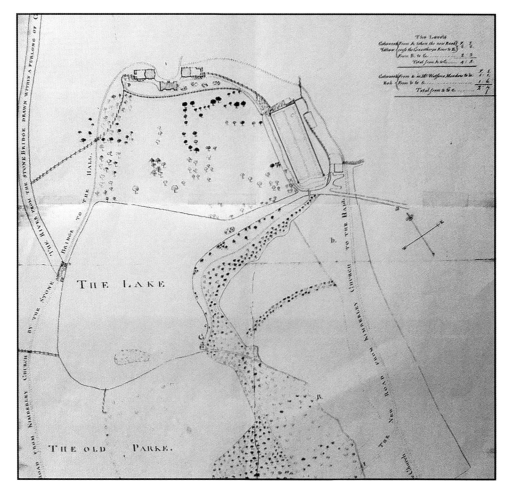

Figure 23.
'Plan of the Lake and Plantations &c belonging to Sʳ John Wodehouse'. Detail on microfilm of a survey by S. King, 1778. (Norfolk Record Office. MF/RO 499/2)

Figure 24.
Kimberley by Humphry Repton c.1780. Pencil, pen and ink, and wash, one of a series of drawings of Norfolk seats and views made by Repton in 1779 and 1780. (Courtesy of Norfolk Museums Service: Norwich Castle Museum & Art Gallery)

The new approach to the hall from the west that Brown proposed in his 1762 plan is shown on both the 1777 and 1778 surveys, crossing the river Tiffey via a stone bridge. Interestingly, although slightly confusingly, the 1777 plan marks this as 'The Old Road from Kimberley Church before the Bridge Fell to the Hall', and shows a ruined bridge, whereas the 1778 plan shows the bridge complete and the road marked 'The Old Road from Kimberley Church by the Stone Bridge to the Hall'. By the nineteenth century the stone bridge was gone and only a footbridge remained, but it would seem to have had a very short life if it had indeed collapsed even before Brown returned to Kimberley in 1778.

Although there is no mention of levelling or smoothing the contours of the lawn in Brown's accounts, it may well be that this, along with work on drainage, formed part of the 'improvements' he carried out at Kimberley. Certainly, several brick, barrel drains exist beneath the lawn, seen by various members of the family and estate workers over the years and, although the hall already stood on rising ground overlooking the lake, the lawn may have required further sculpting to achieve the perfect prospect.

Brown's plan of 1778

Sir Armine died in 1777 and, prior to this, the last payment made to Brown was in 1773, so it would appear that all the work proposed under the first plan, that Sir Armine chose to implement, had been completed by then. Brown's return to Kimberley was at the behest of Sir Armine's successor, Sir John Wodehouse, 6th Baronet (1741–1834). Like so many of his family before him, Sir John served the county in Parliament, in 1784, 1790 and 1796, before being created 1st Baron Wodehouse of Kimberley in 1797. Following his father, he served as a colonel in the East Norfolk Militia from 1774 to 1798. In 1769 he had married Sophia, daughter and heiress of Charles Berkeley of Bruton in Somerset, which added to the Wodehouse family's wealth with property in and around Falmouth in Cornwall.

Figure 25.
John 1st Lord Wodehouse. Lithograph by W. Hornsby from a drawing by Harriet Gunn, 1824. (© National Portrait Gallery, London)

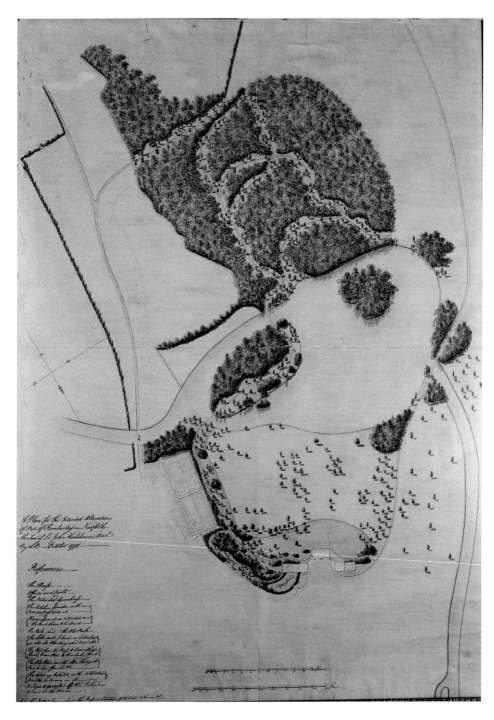

Figure 26.
Brown's second plan for Kimberley, showing intended alterations to part of the park, dated October 1778. (Private Collection. Photo: Roger Last, 2015)

46

Lord Wodehouse's obituary declared that he lived to a 'cheerful and vigorous old age' and was 'firmly attached to the constitution in church and state, unaffectedly religious, and by his own inherent nature a finished gentleman'. [88] Brown's second plan was prepared in 1778 and was entitled 'Intended Plan of the Alterations at Kimberley the Seat of Sir John Wodehouse' (Figure 26). This plan does not cover the whole park but concentrates only on the area around the hall, the kitchen garden and the lake, refining and developing some of the earlier work here. The plan itself has a very distinctive and attractive style, typical of many of Brown's later plans and is likely to have been drawn by John Spyers (1730–1798), who undertook much of Brown's survey work and drafting of plans from 1764. It is both a plan and oblique view, so that trees are shown in elevation, making it easier to identify the different species anticipated.

This plan proposed further changes to the lake and the forming of new pleasure grounds, a greenhouse, drying ground and new walks and drives, as well as the addition of a cross-wall in the kitchen garden. The straight sides of the lake, which apparently survived to this point, were now to be remodelled to simplify the outline. Furthermore, two islands – significantly larger than those proposed in 1762 – were to be added. The larger of the two connected to both the western bank and the southern bank of the lake via footbridges. On the south side of the lake a wood, intersected by winding walks and drives, is depicted. From here another footbridge, spanning the outfall cascade, was to lead out into the park. A photograph of about 1900 shows a wooden bridge in a 'Chinese', mode which might possibly have been designed by Brown (Figure 27).

Figure 27.
One of the wooden footbridges linking the island to the park, from a photograph dated around 1900. (Private Collection)

This is a style he often used but he has not specified how the bridges should look on this plan. The planting proposed for these areas includes, as well as shrubs, ornamental trees drawn as conifers and poplars and, around the lake, weeping willows – species which we do not perhaps usually associate with Brown.

Figure 28.
1778 plan showing the planting scheme on the island, which formed part of the pleasure grounds. Brown's key: F: Pleasure Ground as intended, N: Bridges to go on and off the Island.

Brown had incorporated screening near the kitchen garden in his design of 1762, but the 1778 plan develops this into a long, narrow extension of the new pleasure grounds shown to the east of the hall, flanking a path which continues alongside the kitchen garden and on to one of the islands, continuing via a second bridge to connect with the network of winding tracks in the wood on the south shore of the lake. It is interesting to see that this route was clearly intended to be the one which visitors took to the lake. It would have been perfectly possible – and indeed the

and 31). From these remains it is apparent that the original greenhouse comprised a rear brick wall with a wooden and glass structure attached to the front. In general, the orangeries and greenhouses supplied by Brown were stone or masonry constructions, like those he designed at Redgrave (Suffolk) and at 'Hills' in Horsham (Sussex). It was not unknown for this type of greenhouse to be built in the eighteenth century and John Abercrombie, writing in 1789, describes something quite similar to that at Kimberley:

> Thus, fruit forcing houses, hot-walls &c. for forcing vines and other fruits, &c. to early maturity, are either of different constructions or plans, or occasionally of one general plan for the whole, agreeable to the following observations, all erected in a situation to the sun, having a wall of brickwork &c. behind, with an enclosure of glass sashes before, upright five or six feet high in the front, and sloping above, some formed to work principally by fire, by means of flues, having borders of earth within, in the bottom space, ranged lengthways towards the back part, and sometimes also in front, in which to plant trees.[89]

Behind the greenhouse, built up against its rear wall, are nineteenth-century stables, which incorporate two earlier service buildings. These, and in particular the presence of internal dividing walls, makes it difficult to be certain about the arrangement of the flues in the greenhouse wall, and of their date. One flue is clearly visible behind the centre of the rear wall (marked F on the plan in Figure 32), and this might date from Brown's design, although it is possibly a nineteenth-century addition. Alternatively, there could originally have been two flues, their presence indicated by vertical joints visible in the main central arch, one of which can also be seen inside the stables, although the other now hidden by an internal wall. These earlier flues would have had stoke-holes or fireplaces at their base, however, there is no obvious evidence of these on the rear side of the greenhouse wall.

A greenhouse appears in this location on the Ordnance Survey First Edition 25-inch map of the 1880s. Although the feature shown may have been a nineteenth-century construction, utilising the original rear wall, it is also possible that this is Brown's original greenhouse, by this time around 100 years old and probably much repaired, but still as designed. The greenhouse was sited so that it would have been the first feature to be seen on taking the walk through the pleasure grounds. A guide of 1829 notes that:

> The Pleasure Ground facing the greenhouse, is prettily arranged. On the front of this building is a fine Judas tree, *(Cercis Siliquastrum)*, and the hothouses, &c., under the care of Mr Cooke, are worthy [of] observation.[90]

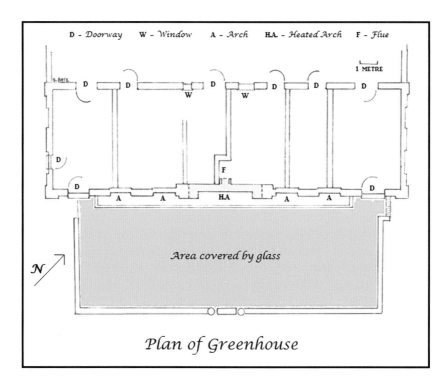

D - Doorway   W - Window   A - Arch   H.A. - Heated Arch   F - Flue

1 METRE

Area covered by glass

N

Plan of Greenhouse

Figure 32.
*Plan of Brown's greenhouse at Kimberley, the hollow section (coloured yellow) heated by air rising from the fire kept continuously lit at **F**. or possibly two earlier flues on either side. (Drawing: Sally Bate, 2016)*

Figure 33.
Remains of the rear wall of Brown's greenhouse. (Photo: Roger Last, 2015)

The kitchen garden was established sometime after the new house, designed by Talman, was erected in the early eighteenth century. It does not appear on the 1714 survey of Kimberley by James Anderton, and the area it later occupied would at that time have been divided across two fields, 'The Strawberry Close' and the 'Cow Pasture'. It first appears on the c.1755 plan by Nollorth, lying around 200m south-east of the hall. By this time the 'Gardens and Orchard' marked on the 1714 plan had been swept away and replaced by a simpler, semi-geometric landscape design around the hall. It seems likely that the original gardens were thought old-fashioned sometime in the 1730s or 1740s and the changes made to establish something more up-to-date also included the construction of a new kitchen garden.

It is usually assumed that Brown's practice was to place kitchen gardens at some distance from the house and out of sight of approach drives, and that he was hostile to all walled gardens and keen to remove them as far as possible from the house. In fact, as noted in the opening chapter, the reality is more complicated and the places at which he worked in Norfolk certainly suggest a more pragmatic approach.

Figure 34.
The south-west half of the kitchen garden looking towards Brown's heated cross-wall.
(Photo: Kate Minnis, 2015)

The existing kitchen garden at Kimberley was large, covering around 1.2 hectares (3 acres), and occupying ground that sloped from the north-west to south-east, where it was bounded by a roughly rectangular pond. High red-brick walls make up the other three sides, the west and east walls ending with brick piers in a distinctly Baroque style. The side walls are topped by dentilated brickwork on the outsides (some missing, probably where later repairs were carried out), unusual decoration for a functional feature. All this seems to suggest that the kitchen garden was intended to be viewed by visitors to Kimberley right from the time it was first built.

The Nollorth plan shows that the interior of the garden was divided by paths into four quarters, but otherwise comprised one continuous open space. Brown proposed the addition of a central 'hot' wall, marked on the plan as 'Intended Cross Wall', dividing its area into two. This heated wall would have been for the benefit of wall-trained, tender fruit trees such as peaches, nectarines, figs and cherries, and would also have introduced what, at the time, was a relatively new and novel feature to the garden.

Figure 35.
Stoke-holes on the north side of the cross-wall, now bricked up. (Photo: Roger Last, 2015)

Figure 36.
Gateway through Brown's cross-wall in the kitchen garden. (Photo: Roger Last, 2015)

Brown's wall is, like the external walls, built of red brick and has a central door and archway between brick piers capped in stone and decorated with small ball finials. On the north side are two pairs of stoke-holes, now bricked up, one pair on each side of the doorway. Each stoke-hole is 30 cm (12 inches) wide and the pairs are 35 cm (14 inches) apart; their size indicates they would have been fired with coal rather than wood. The system of internal heating flues is clearly visible on the south elevation where there are three courses of bricks laid on their sides and spaced evenly up the height of the wall.

Kimberley was already a well-established site where tree-planting had been carried out for several centuries before Brown first visited in the 1760s. In such a case he would have taken advantage of existing planting, making changes and creating new planting schemes where appropriate. In the park to the north-east of the hall there are examples of very large oak trees, many pollarded, which must pre-date Brown. Some of these ancient trees follow the line of old field boundaries and 'hollow ways' and are amongst the oldest in the county.

Figure 37.
View of Kimberley Hall from across the lake, with planting much matured since Brown worked on the site. Engraving by J. Grieg from a drawing by John Sell Cotman for Excursions through Norfolk, 1818, this version taken from an early 20th-century postcard. (Private Collection)

Grigor in 1841 talks of 'old blasted oaks, sapless and silent spectacles, yet beautiful withal, of the grandest decay we can witness in vegetable life' in the park at the entrance to Kimberley and criticises the treatment of the oaks which have been 'so unmercifully topped'.[91]   Of the view from the house he declares: 'Its lawn is magnificent, and well furnished with grand old trees: it contains many open views in which the picturesque is prominent, and anon those which are stamped with deep woodland solemnity'.[92]   In a view of the hall from across the lake, John Sell Cotman depicted clumps of mature trees and a wooded island in his early nineteenth-century engraving, the result of Brown's planting. (Figure 37)

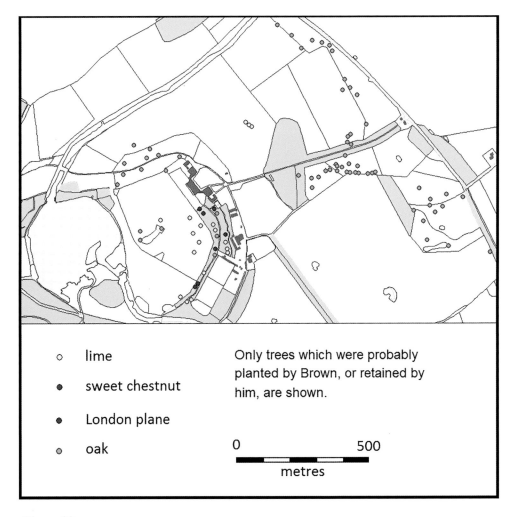

○	lime	Only trees which were probably planted by Brown, or retained by him, are shown.
●	sweet chestnut	
●	London plane	
◉	oak	

0   500

metres

Figure 38.
Plan of trees in Kimberley Park, which were likely to have been introduced by Brown, or which pre-date his work. (Survey by Norfolk Gardens Trust's research group, 2015)

A recent tree survey in the park has highlighted the trees which are likely to have been planted by Brown as well as those surviving from earlier periods (Figure 38). Amongst the latter, attention should be drawn to a number of oaks and limes in the area lying between the hall and the lake. These are larger than would be expected for mid-eighteenth-century plantings, and presumably represent specimens already mature when Brown came to Kimberley, and retained by him as part of his landscape improvements. These older trees can be distinguished from those – such as a group of three limes to the north-east of the hall, with girths of between 4.2 metres and 6 metres – whose size suggests that they date from Brown's time.

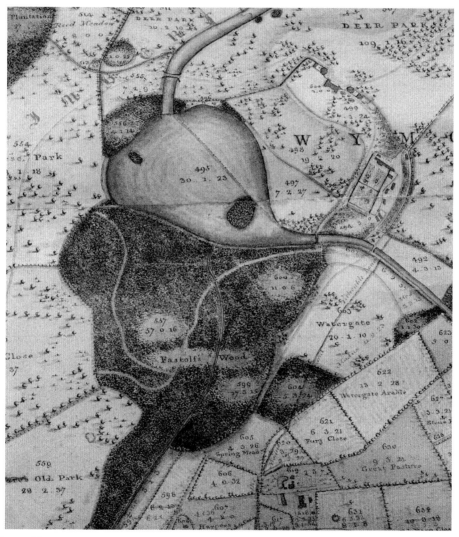

Figure 39.
Detail from 'The Kimberley and Litcham Estates of the Right Hon. Lord Wodehouse' map dated 1827. (Norfolk Record Office: MC 2372/1. Photo: Roger Last)

Other trees almost certainly planted by Brown display smaller girths, however, their growth rates reduced because they have been growing close together. These trees are all clearly shown on the first 6-inch Ordnance Survey map; they would have been little more than 100 years old at this time.

To ascertain how many of Brown's 'improvements' were implemented, we can study the maps which depict the park in the years that followed, such as an estate map surveyed in 1827 (Figure 39). These show how the outline of the lake was made more natural, much along the lines that Brown proposed in 1778, and that the larger island was added and survived into the nineteenth century. The greenhouse was built, as was the heated cross-wall in the kitchen garden. The wood to the south of the lake appears on the Ordnance Survey maps of the 1880s, marked as 'Great Carr'. It is larger in area than that on Brown's plan but is still today threaded with paths.

Kimberley after Brown

Less than ten years after Brown's last work at Kimberley, Sir John was again seeking to make alterations to the lake. He approached John Hare, otherwise unknown as a landscape designer, who had worked for the Wodehouse family as land agent at their Lexham estate. He supervised the works carried out to divert a public highway to allow the expansion of that estate, to judge from a payment in 1775 of £78 to Mr. Hare 'on Acct for making new road'.[93] Hare's rather startling 1786 design, looking more like an abstract painting than a surveyed drawing, shows four islands in the lake, one large and three smaller (Figure 40). The outline of the south and east sides of the lake were to be altered and the course of the river changed; and the circuit path was to go across the river, so that the large island was not included as part of the walk.

The plan was not carried out but it seems surprising that, given Brown's long association with Kimberley and his reputation, Sir John was quite happy to think about changing his plans just a decade after his work here had been completed, and only three years after Brown's death. It shows that Brown's work was not always viewed by contemporaries with the respect and reverence that we give it today.

Sir John appears to have made few further changes to the landscape at Kimberley although he was able to take advantage of early nineteenth-century enclosures to expand the park. Crownthorpe parish was enclosed in 1778 and by 1797 much of the common had been incorporated into the park; Wymondham was enclosed in 1810, allowing expansion east towards the Carleton Forehoe Road. It was around this time that the bridge crossing the river Tiffey on the Wymondham to Carleton Forehoe Road was built. It has three arches constructed of brick and stone, and was built in 1815 by Francis Stone of Norwich at a cost of £900.[94] Its design is similar to, albeit simpler than, that of a bridge which Brown provided at Burghley in Cambridgeshire.

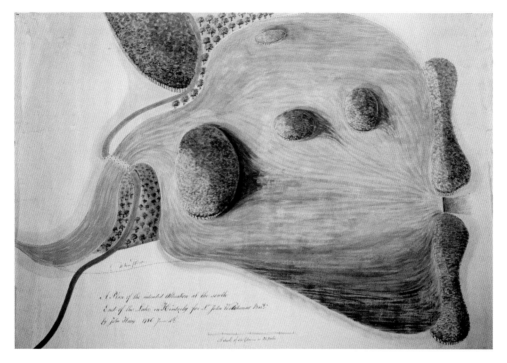

Figure 40.
Plan of intended alterations to the south end of the lake, prepared by John Hare for Sir John Wodehouse and dated 4 June 1786. (Private Collection. Photo: Roger Last, 2015)

Tree planting on the estate continued; an inventory of timber made at the death of Sir John in 1834 shows mainly oak, ash and beech plantations.[95] Although some trees within the park were probably planted by Brown many, including examples of beech, ash and London plane, are likely to be of nineteenth-century date, established in Sir John's time and later.

Sometime in the early nineteenth century an ice house was built just outside the north wall of the kitchen garden, the remains of which survive. The ice house was built of brick with a tunnel-vaulted passageway leading to the shaft with a domed roof.

John, 2nd Baron Wodehouse, succeeded in 1834 and the following year engaged the architect Anthony Salvin to make alterations to the hall, including adding the quadrant passages linking the detached offices to the main house. Salvin also made

Figure 41.
View of Kimberley Hall and the lake c.1860s by Alexander Francis Lydon and taken from Seats of the Noblemen and Gentlemen of Great Britain and Ireland, edited by F.O. Morris. (Private Collection)

some changes to the facades and rearranged the interiors of the hall, work continuing until 1838.[96] By this time there was a terrace along the front of the house, about 200 yards in length, which Grigor describes as 'well executed and . . . unquestionably an improvement'. He was less impressed, however, with the flower garden at the western end of the terrace which was 'after the old formal Dutch style, but capable of great improvement'. He goes on to dismiss Dutch gardens as consisting 'chiefly in having moats and ditches; and in flower-plats, symmetry and smoothness' and with 'little pieces of lawn' which are 'usually intersected with canals of mud'.[97]

The layout of the terrace, including the retaining wall, was designed by William Andrews Nesfield, a leading landscape designer of the period. Nesfield was Salvin's brother-in-law and worked with him on many of his commissions, so it is likely that Nesfield was introduced to Baron Wodehouse by Salvin.[98] The Nesfield archives give the dates for the design and construction of the terrace as 1847 onwards, so it seems that a terrace was already in place which Nesfield redesigned and improved[99] (Figure 42).

Figure 42.
The formal terrace to the south-west of the hall, laid out by W. A. Nesfield. This view shows the parterre planted with bedding plants some fifty years after Nesfield's work. The distinctive style of retaining wall, topped with urns, is likely to be of his design. (Postcard c.1900. Image Courtesy of Norfolk County Council Library and Information Service)

Later Wodehouse descendants seem to have made few changes to the landscape, something which has helped to preserve much of Brown's work. John, 2nd Baron Wodehouse, died in 1846 and was succeeded by his grandson, also John, whose highly successful diplomatic career probably left him little time for improving the estate. He served in every Liberal government of the second half of the nineteenth century in roles including Lord Lieutenant of Ireland, Lord Privy Seal, Colonial Secretary, Indian Secretary and foreign secretary under Lord Rosebery.[100] In 1866 he was created First Earl Kimberley. His son John, who succeeded as 2nd Earl Kimberley in 1902, was rather less successful politically, arguing with both the Tory and Liberal parties. Two of his sons, Philip and Edward, were killed in the First World War and his remaining son, John, became 3rd Earl in 1932. On his death in an air raid in 1941, his son John inherited at the age of sixteen and was to become the last of the Wodehouses to live at Kimberley.[101]

One addition to the gardens at Kimberley in the early twentieth century was a rose garden, created for Lady Isabel, wife of the 2nd Lord Kimberley, in a walled area adjacent to the kitchen garden. Contemporary photographs show the garden with a

61

rustic shelter in one corner, from which to sit and enjoy the colourful flower beds (Figure 43).

Figure 43.
Rose Garden c.1912. The figure in the photograph is thought to be Lady Isabel, wife of the 2nd Lord Kimberley. The garden is also known as 'Isabel's Garden'. (Private Collection. Photo: Roger Last, 2015)

Kimberley Hall was occupied by the army during the Second World War and suffered greatly as a result. The £10,000 compensation paid by the Ministry of Works paid for repairs, including reroofing, and for alterations by James Fletcher-Watson who created the present entrance hall and opened up the central window on the north-east front to form a doorway with a portico on Ionic columns.[102] The estate was sold by the 4th Earl of Kimberley in 1958 and split up. The hall and its surrounding parkland were bought by Ronald Buxton, in whose family's ownership it belongs to day.

Figure 44.
Kimberley Hall, north-east front, showing the wings, originally detached, which were linked to the main house by Anthony Salvin in the 1830s. Also the entrance and portico, added by James Fletcher-Watson in the 1950s. (Photo: ©Mike Page Aerial Photography)

The significance of Brown's work at Kimberley

Many of the features created by Brown can still be seen at Kimberley. The view from the hall still looks down across the sloping lawns towards the lake, although twentieth-century silting has reduced the size of the latter and changed its outline so that the island is no longer distinct. The rear wall of the greenhouse remains, as does the 'hot wall' dividing the kitchen garden, and the route through the pleasure grounds down towards the lake, although now through woodland rather than Brown's shrubbery, can still be followed in part.

Although best known today for use of indigenous and naturalised species like oak, beech and lime, the planting he proposed for Kimberley show him using a much wider range of trees appropriate to different situations. In the area between the hall and lake and in the wider parkland he used conifers among the deciduous trees, and edging the lake he introduced weeping willows and poplars. Many of these trees are shorter lived than oak and beech and so have now disappeared. The pleasure ground and shrubbery, too, are likely to have included a wide variety of shrubs. The siting of the pleasure ground very close to the kitchen garden, so that the latter was included as part of the intended walk down to the lake, is also interesting in showing that Brown was prepared to make it one of the features for visitors, perhaps showing off the new 'hot wall' as part of the tour?

Although not all of Brown's proposals for Kimberley were adopted, the work he did for the Wodehouse family thus sheds important new light on his design philosophy and challenges some of the received ideas about what a Brown landscape should be. Above all, Kimberley Park still evokes a very Brownian landscape to this day, and remains the best preserved of his designs in Norfolk.

Figure 45.
View of the lake from the roof of Kimberley Hall, a typical Brownian landscape. (Photo: Roger Last, 2015)

CHAPTER 3   LANGLEY

Langley Park (Photo: ©Mike Page Aerial Photography)

Introduction

The village of Langley lies roughly 10 miles (16 kilometres) to the south-east of Norwich, to the north of the main road to Loddon. Langley Park extends over a long, low hill of light gravelly soil some 90 feet (27 metres) above sea level, surrounded to the south and east by the marshes and water-meadows around the confluence of the rivers Yare and the Chet, and to the north by the alder-carrs of the Thurton brook. Towards Carleton St Peter the hill has some pleasing undulations, but the area of the park is fairly level, sloping gently down from the house towards the west. The house itself is, like Kimberley Hall, a red-brick eighteenth-century building with prominent corner towers, and with flanking pavilions which are connected to the main building by curving corridors. Today it is the home of Langley School, an independent boarding establishment.

A Premonstratensian Abbey was established on the edge of the marshes in the late twelfth century, known as Langley Abbey. Its lands were acquired by the Berney family (pronounced Barney) following the Dissolution in the 1530s, consisting at the time of nearly a thousand acres within the parishes of Langley, Chedgrave, Hardley, Carleton, Thurton and Bergh Apton. The Berneys had considerable holdings in the county and by the early seventeenth century were considered to be

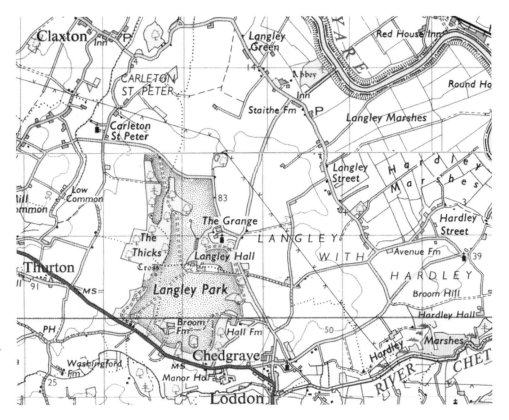

Figure 46.
Location map for Langley Park (Reproduced from the Ordnance Survey 1 inch 7th Series 1955–61 map with kind permission of the Ordnance Survey)

'the greatest family next the lords' in Norfolk. When Richard Berney was granted a baronetcy in 1620 he was thought to be worth about '£7,000 per annum and £50,000 in money', but he left his fortune away from the title, to another son who squandered the lot.[103] There were however many grandsons, and Richard, the second son of John Berney of Westwick Hall, inherited what remained of the Langley estate in the early eighteenth century. He became a barrister and was briefly an MP, and finally became Recorder of Norwich. Whenever he could, he augmented the estate through further acquisitions.[104]

The building of Langley Hall

In 1733 Richard Berney's only child Elizabeth married Thomas Bramston MP and within the year they had a son, Thomas Berney Bramston. Dynastic thoughts may have prompted the idea of building a fine new house at Langley. Berney picked a flat site on the south-west end of the low hill, not far from Langley church – where some of his forebears were buried[105] – and the old Abbey grange, in a spot sheltered to the north by Langley Wood, an area of ancient woodland. The land was still occupied in part by unenclosed open fields: an undated parish map survives which shows the outline of the proposed new building and two central avenues, using dotted lines (Figure 47).

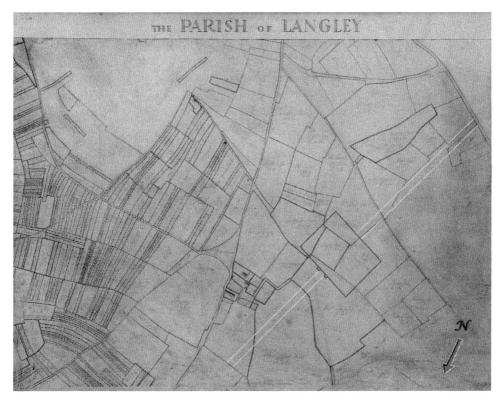

Figure 47.
Langley parish map of the 1730s showing strip fields and in faint dotted lines (highlighted)
the proposed site for the new hall. The footprint of the gardens is marked in red and the
two main avenues in light green. (Mrs Frances Kirkpatrick. Photo: Roger Last, 2016)

Just as the project was nearing completion, it became clear that Berney was completely out of funds. In October 1736 he transferred the Langley estate to his son-in-law, partly in lieu of his daughter's marriage settlement – which had promised to be splendid – and partly to pay his creditors. A mountain of debts came to light. 'Surprising vanity of one who passed for a wise man, and a great lawyer,' ran the parliamentary report, 'to affect the reputation of a great estate when he knew he was poor!'[106] Having made a will in 1737, following a period of poor health, Berney died soon after. His son-in-law had no option but to get what he could from a quick sale of Langley. The debts amounted to some £55,000 and the list of creditors was long.

The sale document appears to have been written during Berney's lifetime, perhaps when seeking a mortgage. The mansion was described as:

> A commodious pleasant seat for a Gentleman lately built after the newest manner & with very good and convenient offices thereto belonging, with near nine acres of garden & nursery grounds well planted with all sorts of fruit trees with large and convenient yards and walks leading to the said house.

The deer park, an indispensable sign of gentility, was of a modest size:

> 95 acres of land enclosed with pales, 60 acres and part thereof is a fine thick piece of pasture ground well supplied with water with a large number of oak timber trees ornamental to the view of the house growing thereon, being thriving trees in Mr. Berney's own use.[107]

The park appears to have included Langley Wood, to the north and north-west of the hall. The agent reckoned that the property's value, between £5,000 and £6,000, could be best realised in 'Materials to be pulled down and sold off the premises as in fact it appears to me of no more worth'.[108]

Tempting as this suggestion might be to modern tastes, the buyer had other plans. George Proctor, lately returned from Venice where he held a diplomatic office as the British Resident, was one of Berney's many mortgagors. He had seen the place being built and liked it enough in February 1738 to give £30,000 for the estate, plus one-shilling stamp duty. He gave a grant to the widow Berney, and immediately set out to finish the project properly, putting in hand both interior and exterior works. He laid out avenues to the north and south of the house in the axial manner of the early eighteenth century. Within a fortnight Proctor's agent John Lows was advising him of rents collected from tenants at Langley, Hardley, Chedgrave, Carleton and Buckenham, and refers to 'the materials carried from your house which were to finish the building with the Locks etc taken from the Doors . . . I will get the Cost information as to their number and value.' Lows also describes what they were doing in the park: 'The avenue leading to the House is planted through with oaks, and where the land was light and sandy I carried good earth to plant in, that it might be as uniform as could be made.'[109]

An undated map of around 1738, which survives only as a microfilm copy in the Norfolk Record Office, shows the landscape as it was around this time. The house is represented by a rectangular block, with the present kitchen garden located 140 metres to the south-east, flanked on its western side by service yards. The house was approached from an eastern entrance, on what is now Staithe Road/Langley Road, along a relatively narrow avenue, not axially aligned with the house – this still survives as the main approach to the school. To the north of the house, double rectangles divided into geometric shapes, ranged either side of a central open vista, appear to represent formal gardens – probably parterres of grass and gravel close to the house and 'wildernesses' – areas of ornamental shrubbery/woodland – with typical 'St Andrew's Cross' arrangements of allées, beyond (Figure 48). Traces of these features can be seen on aerial photographs held at the Historic Environment Record at Gressenhall.[110] To the north of these gardens lay the substantial 24-hectare (60-acre) area of Langley Wood, through which the central vista running north from the hall was continued in the form of an avenue. This axial vista was also extended to the south of the hall, here taking the form of a much wider avenue, framing the full width of the house, which continued for some 1,200 metres (1,312 yards) as far as the road from Norwich to Loddon and Chedgrave. Halfway along its length this southern vista was crossed by the old road from Thurton to Chedgrave. This was closed later in the eighteenth century, although its line is still maintained as a series of field boundaries. The southern portion of this avenue would have run through enclosed fields, but the northern section passed through the deer park, mentioned above in the sales document of 1737. The pales are carefully detailed on the map.

Figure 48.
Map (c.1738) showing the original formal garden and the north avenue cut through Langley Wood. This image has been created digitally combining two microfilm slides, the whereabouts of the water-damaged originals are now unknown. (Norfolk Record Office: Mf/RO 120/7 nos. 90 and 92)

For the interiors of the hall, George Proctor wanted the best money could buy. Elaborate plasterwork on the staircase, library and saloon is attributed to Charles Stanley, who was working in England until 1746.[111] The decorative schemes are remarkable in remaining, on the whole, unchanged since their inauguration, even to the original paintings set into the plasterwork. The amateur sculptor Sir Henry Cheere is thought to have carved the chimney piece in the library (stolen in the early twenty-first century) and another in the study, with details of a fox, pig and rabbit, identified as very similar to one of Cheere's at Picton Castle in Pembrokeshire.[112] Proctor, who was a bachelor, had an eclectic and extensive art collection, much of it acquired in Venice, including Roman and French bronzes, funerary urns, Renaissance and contemporary statues, as well as many fine Old Master paintings and drawings, and as the rooms became ready they were quickly filled.

Figure 49.
Detail from a portrait of George Proctor. (Private Collection. Photo: Roger Last, 2015)

It is not known how much of the work put in hand by George Proctor was completed in the six years that he owned Langley before he died. However, he instilled considerable discernment in the decorative arts in his nephew (and heir)

70

William Beauchamp (1722–1773). William's mother Anne was George Proctor's sister, and his father Thomas Beauchamp was the only son of a respected philanthropist and Freeman of the City of London, Ephraim Beauchamp. The Beauchamps lived at White Hall, a recently built stucco mansion off White Hart Lane in Tottenham in Middlesex. Thomas Beauchamp died falling from his horse while William was still an infant, leaving him the sole inheritor of Ephraim Beauchamp's fortune, which included valuable investments and 330 acres of land round Tottenham and Edmonton, with houses and market gardens.[113] George Proctor's other sister Jane married Christopher Tower, and all three siblings inherited jointly from their father, William Proctor of Epsom. William was thus, from his earliest years, well supported by both the Beauchamp and the Proctor fortunes, and now in 1744, aged twenty-two, he inherited Langley Park.

The Beauchamp-Proctors
George Proctor's will stipulated that William should add the Proctor name and arms to his own.[114] Like many young men with funds, William Beauchamp-Proctor had friends at court, and only a year later he acquired a baronetcy. Sponsored by Lord Bute, William Pitt and the Duke of Newcastle, he was subsequently put forward in 1747 as the uncontested Whig candidate for Middlesex, regardless of inclination and ability. An anonymous constituent, who came to know William well over the twenty years that he represented Middlesex, later described his one and only speech in the House:

> Though surrounded by your friends, and prepared for the occasion, you could only get out – 'Gentlemen – a – I thank you – a – gentlemen' and then loud enough to be heard by many near you, you beat your hand on the partition before you, crying – 'What must I say next? – What must I say next?' Some other inarticulate and unconnected words did follow; but your friends, to cover your insufficiency and relieve your distress set up a loud huzza, and so concluded your address. [115]

William may have been more taken up with his recent marriage and the building works on the house than with political matters. Prudently, to reduce any leaching of Proctor funds outside the family, he had married his first cousin Jane Tower, daughter of Jane Proctor.

John Wootton was commissioned to paint the Beauchamp-Proctors and friends at Langley shortly after the marriage (Figure 50) and his work shows, in the background, a two-storey, red-brick house of five bays flanked by two separate seven-bay pavilions. The stable block is clearly seen to the right, with Langley church tower above the trees. The figures appear to be pausing on Oakley Common Road, the old route to Chedgrave from Thurton, which at this time formed the southern boundary of the park. Framing the group is the broad southern

Figure 50.
The Beauchamp-Proctor Family by John Wootton c.1749 with house in background.
(Courtesy of Norfolk Museums Service, Castle Museum)

avenue, now eleven years old, which is shown as double-planted and with paths running between the trees. According to John Harris, Wootton's interest lay more in the composition of the group than in precise depiction of architecture, the job of the house being to signify social standing. A Palladian rotunda is shown amongst trees near the hall, but this is no guarantee that one existed. Many prospects of this sort, as Harris has noted, are ornamented with quite substantial temples and follies that were never built.[116] Nonetheless it is clear that Langley Hall was not yet of its present size and height, as Wootton could hardly have omitted such obvious features as the corner towers, when his patron gestures towards it so emphatically.

There is considerable conjecture about the date of the modifications to Berney's original house which gave it something approaching its modern appearance, but the Wootton painting indicates that the major remodelling works must have been carried out after 1749, and therefore by William Beauchamp-Proctor rather than George Proctor. Matthew Brettingham, the executive architect at Holkham, may have been involved but to what extent is unclear. Letter and bills for work at Langley from John Sanderson (d 1774) describe internal alterations in 1757; he had worked with Sanderson Miller at Hagley in Warwickshire and with Thomas Prowse at Kimberley in 1755–7; he had also worked with Charles Stanley and Sir Henry Cheere on other projects. Langley as it appears today certainly resembles both Kimberley and Hagley Hall, right up to the weathervanes on the square towers.[117] Pevsner too thinks that John Sanderson was involved.[118] Langley also has a rare example of the work of Andien de Clermont, who left England in 1755, in the form of a whimsical rococo ceiling for the boudoir, which is still in place.[119] Sir William commissioned some first-class furniture for specific positions in the house from makers such as Hallett, Vile and Chippendale.[120] Portraits of William's many children were made by Opie, Romney and Reynolds, and landscapes by Wilson, Stubbs and Gainsborough were added to his uncle's collection.

A pair of remarkable paintings of Langley Hall, long housed elsewhere, have recently come to light, showing prospects of the north and south fronts. They contain intriguing depictions of the park and grounds, but their veracity is not beyond question. The artist and date are not inscribed on them, but stylistically they are of the mid-eighteenth century, probably from sometime in the 1750s. The prospect of the north front (Figure 51) indicates clearly the darker tone of the brickwork in the corner towers and second storey, compared with that of the original, central core. It also shows an architectural feature that is not now to be seen, consisting of a pair of long flanking walls with pedimented, brick niches for statuary ending in substantial gate piers with double ironwork gates. The only evidence on the ground to corroborate these massive walls is the slight elevation of the terraced area on the north front, extending beyond each tower to a point aligned to the outer edges of the two pavilions (measuring 19 metres), just as shown in the painting. Being just a little higher than the present lawn, three shallow steps are required at each end of this terrace to take the existing gravel walk across the width of the whole garden. However, a short section of wall still stands on both sides of the main block, each housing a pedimented brick niche. Are these walls the remnants of the wider structures on the painting or were they not built to the full width shown? Today, one wall screens a single-storey extension on the west side, the other balancing it on the east side, allowing space behind it for a sheltered garden near the library and garden gallery.

There is documentary evidence of a need to build a larger dining room soon after 1761 when Sir William's first wife Jane died, in the same year that he was appointed a Knight of the Order of the Bath in the Coronation Honours of George III. In 1762 he married again, finding with Laetitia Johnson a useful dowry of £25,000, following which he commissioned Thomas Bardwell (d. 1767) to paint full-length portraits of himself in his ceremonial robes, his new wife Laetitia and his late parents. To accommodate these a larger dining room was built onto the west end which needed screening walls to avoid imbalance of the north front. A third piece of evidence is a 1765 bill from Hallett for a set of dining chairs.[121]

Figure 51.
Undated oil painting, probably from the mid-1750s, of the north prospect of Langley by an unknown artist (Private collection, photo: Roger Last, 2016)

Over the mantelpiece there is a fine portrait of George Proctor from the 1730s, likely to have hung previously in another room. It seems then that a date span of 1763–5 for the construction of the new dining room is more likely than Pevsner's suggestion of the 1840s but supports his suspicion that some features of it may have been moved from elsewhere in the house.

The area of garden and park shown on the painting of the north front includes part of the grounds that the Beauchamp-Proctors later employed Brown to improve. Deer stand among mature trees outside the garden area, and allées can be made out within the geometrical wildernesses in the foreground. Nearer the house the earlier formal parterres have already been erased leaving two squares of regularly planted young trees, painted simply, almost crudely, in contrast to renditions of the mature trees, and leaving between them an expanse of lawn similar to a stage set, empty apart from a pony pulling a roller across it.

Figure 52.
Undated oil painting, probably from the mid-1750s, of the south prospect of Langley by an unknown artist (Private collection, photo: Roger Last, 2016)

The household offices and stable block are totally hidden by mature woodland, and the church is half-hidden by trees. However, the most surprising feature of this garden view is a shady canal with trimmed banks, tucked below the raised foreground, stretching across the whole width of the painting, its presence accentuated by the reflection from an urn on a plinth placed near the edge. There is one piece of corroborative evidence for this canal, prior to Brown's visit, in the shape of a narrow, rectangular feature marked north of the formal garden's wildernesses on the 1738 map in Figure 48. This could have been the canal but there is no sign of it today.

The south prospect (Figure 52) shows the main block of the house with its 1740s improvements and its two pavilions, but the artist does not make clear whether these are still separate or now linked to the main house. The gravel sweep and white bollards featured in the Wootton painting are clearly shown. The double avenue has, however, been removed and replaced by lines of paired clumps. The trees appear mature: the clumps could have been formed by leaving sections of avenue standing, augmented by setting additional trees around them, but may again have been a planned improvement rather than an accurate representation of features actually in place at the time. The inclusion of proposed additions to the landscape is suggested by other features shown on the paintings. In both prospects a temple with a pediment and four columns is sketched in a rather ghostly form, lightly suspended over the grass, free of base or steps. The south prospect has in addition a rather densely painted white flint cottage with a narrow central gable, placed on a non-existent rise south-west of the house, roughly where a stone cross now stands. These are most likely to be proposals, and of a somewhat whimsical character, although like the clumped avenue they may suggest that there was an interest on the part of the family in developing the park and pleasure grounds in accordance with the fashion for a simpler and more 'natural' style which became current in the 1740s and 1750s.

Figure 53.
Detail of Sir William Beauchamp-Proctor in his ceremonial robes of the Order of the Bath. (Private collection. Photo: Roger Last, 2015)

76

Lancelot Brown's design for Langley

When Dorothy Stroud[122] visited Langley in 1974 the plan by Brown, known to exist, could not be traced. Much of the parkland had by then been cleared for arable farming, and no Brownian features were obvious. However, today the original plan, inscribed to Sir William Beauchamp-Proctor, signed 'L.B. 1765', is still in the building (Figure 54) and a copy on microfiche is held at the Norfolk Records Office.[123] The drawing is in pen and ink, not rendered with colour, and clearly indicates soft and hardwood trees in the planting detail. The plan shows the position of the stables, stack-yard and kitchen garden but does not indicate the west dining room on the footprint of the house. It is a fine example of Brown's style, as this was maturing through the early 1760s.

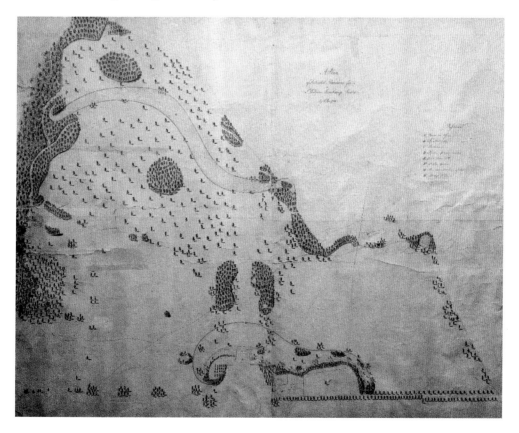

Figure 54.
Lancelot Brown's Plan for Langley, 1765. (Private collection, photo: Roger Last, 2015)

The plan deals, not with the entire landscape around the hall, but only with the area lying to the north; even the main area of the enclosed deer park, to the south of the house, is omitted. This in itself is not unusual – Brown's plans often (as at

Kimberley in 1778) dealt with only a small portion of the landscape around a great house. The restricted focus suggests that Brown, and presumably Sir William Beauchamp-Proctor, had two main concerns: the removal of the wildernesses, and other geometric features, in the area immediately to the north of the house; and the expansion of the park to the north-west, at the expense of Langley Wood.

Figure 55.
Annotated section of Brown's plan. The faint dots showing the existing garden layout have been highlighted in yellow and the house shaded in red.

Brown proposed removing the avenue and modifying the wildernesses or bosquets in the area to the north of the house, blurring any straight lines with additional planting round the edges and filling in the allées or vistas cut through them, thus converting them into large informal clumps. Faintly drawn on his plan (Figure 55) – with dotted lines – traces of the earlier formal garden can be seen, apparently including the canal lying to the north of the wildernesses, giving further credence to the representation of the garden included on the undated north prospect of the house shown in Figure 51. In place of this grand, geometric setting, an elegant, informal pleasure ground, ranged roughly east–west, was to be laid out to the north of the house, wrapping round it to the west and south-west, and separated from the adjacent parkland by a curving ha-ha (Figure 56). The pleasure ground comprised an area of lawn with trees, which are shown on the plan as both deciduous and coniferous. These were to be scattered singly and grouped into clumps. Brown drew an oval belt of trees round the north and east of the service area to the south-east of the hall, sweeping round with a further section on the southern side of the east drive, shielding the stable block from the lower park. His drawing of the kitchen garden shows it divided into four sections with a tree in the middle.

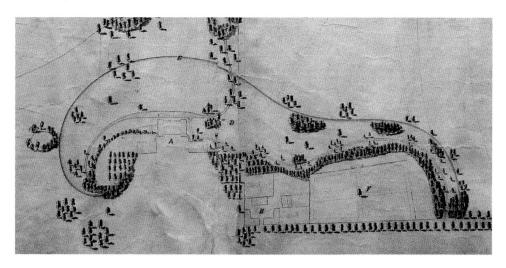

Figure 56.
Detail of Brown's plan showing the long ha-ha (E) and pleasure garden (D) curving around the house (A), stable yard (B) and kitchen garden (F).

A long, serpentine path – presumably dressed with gravel – is shown running northwards from the pleasure ground, crossing the ha-ha, and passing through the eastern clump (converted from one the earlier wildernesses) to the north of the house, before turning east and running through the perimeter belt on the north-eastern margins of the park, ending at the parish church. Sir William and his family were to be provided with private access to the church on Sunday morning – a pleasant stroll through the park. Not all formality was removed from the vicinity

79

of the hall. Brown's plan shows an avenue, lining the old entrance drive leading in from the east: this was presumably retained from the earlier landscape, although whether on Brown's volition, or the owner's, is of course uncertain.

Figure 57.
Detail showing Brown's clumps of trees and the north-west area of the park. Brown has shown an existing rectangular pond (above G) in the centre of the proposed lake. This pond is depicted on later maps and is still present today.

Brown proposed to make the most changes to the area lying to the north-west of the hall where, as already intimated, the park was to be considerably extended in an unusual manner – by incorporating within it the area of Langley Wood, most of which was to be thinned to create a densely treed area of parkland, although some sections were to be retained to form a number of clumps of varying size. In addition, the western and eastern ends of the wood were to be retained and extended with new planting to form a perimeter belt. Winding its way through the blocks of trees is an unsurfaced ride – a typical Brownian feature. This is not clearly delineated (as it is in some Brown plans) where it crosses the open turf, but only when it cuts through clumps and – most clearly – when it runs through the denser woodland (Figure 57).

The most striking new feature Brown proposed to create for Sir William was a serpentine lake, with its ends hidden by groups of trees. Although the rides around it are not surfaced, they are permanent thoroughfares, carefully designed and traversing the lake at its eastern end by means of an ornamental bridge. The tree planting around the bridge is shown to be particularly elaborate, including what are clearly weeping willows. (Figure 58)

Figure 58.
Detail showing the eastern end of the lake, with a bridge (marked H) and several weeping willows reflected in the water.

In the main, the planting shown on Brown's plan within the park is deciduous – the vast majority of the free-standing trees on the plan were, in fact, timber trees which had formerly grown in Langley Wood. But some conifers are depicted in areas and features which were to be newly established: in the north-eastern belt, beside the path to the church; and in the clumps which were to be planted along the park's eastern margins. Moreover, additional weeping willows, other than those just noted by the intended lake bridge, are shown scattered around the margins of the lake.

Langley is in many ways a fairly standard example of Brown's designs from the mid-1760s, with its simple pleasure ground bounded by a ha-ha, curving gravel path, perimeter rides, clumps and belts. However, two features are particularly noteworthy and somewhat unusual. One is the rigidly serpentine outline of the lake, surprisingly abstract when compared with other, near-contemporary designs such as Bowood in Wiltshire's 1763 plan (Figure 4). The other is the way in which the majority of the planting shown on the plan has been derived from – and most of the design created by – drastically thinning a large area of ancient, semi-natural woodland. Such a procedure has some parallels in Brown's work elsewhere, most notably at the slightly earlier Ashridge Park in Hertfordshire where most of the design, including Brown's famous 'Golden Valley', was created by sculpting open areas and clumps out of formerly continuous stands of woodland.

How much of Brown's plan was executed?

It is hard to know precisely how much of Brown's plan for Langley was executed, not least because changes continued to be made to the landscape in the subsequent decades, and no plan of the estate survives from the period between Brown's activities here in the 1760s, and 1816. A brief account therefore needs to be presented of what is known about changes made to the landscape in the late eighteenth and early nineteenth century, in order to evaluate the extent of Brown's contribution.

Even before anything could be done to implement Brown's recommendations, William Beauchamp-Proctor's attention was forcibly taken up by politics. Prior to the 1768 general election Sir William, never contested in Middlesex, was in Norfolk giving support to both Sir Armine Woodhouse of Kimberley and Sir Edward Astley at Melton Constable, whose seats were both being challenged. Then, at the last minute, William's Middlesex constituency received a late entry, none other than Sergeant John Glynn (lawyer to the infamous Radical reformer John Wilkes) who had been excluded by Parliament for questioning cronyism, bribery and malpractice in government. Riots and fighting broke out in Middlesex, but after one of the most tumultuous and troubling elections ever recorded Sir William was defeated, as was Sir Armine Wodehouse in Norfolk. Neither of them stood again. It was rumoured that Sir William spent £10,000 (equivalent to £1.5

million today) on the traditional means of gaining votes, the very principle Glynn was standing against.[124]   Sir William Beauchamp Proctor retired to Langley and died in 1773 aged fifty-one, interred in the family vault at Tottenham beside his first wife Jane Tower.   His widow Laetitia lived on in Upper Grosvenor Street, London until 1798.   She obtained some glass salvaged by a Norwich merchant from Rouen during the French Revolution, and subsequently had the pieces installed in churches around Langley.[125]

Figure 59.
Sir Thomas Beauchamp-Proctor portrait by Benjamin West in 1777. (©Tate, London, 2016)

Sir Thomas Beauchamp-Proctor (1756–1827) succeeded to the family estates aged seventeen, while still at Harrow (Figure 59). In 1778 he married Mary Palmer from Berkshire, a statuesque beauty (Figure 60). It was a year of marriages.

Figure 60.
Mary (Palmer), Lady Beauchamp-Proctor by George Romney in 1782–6. (©Courtesy of the Huntington Art Collection. San Marino, California)

His elder sister Anne (1749–1813) married Sir Edmund Bacon on 29 January 1778, at nearby Raveningham. A younger sister, Frances, married John Custance of Weston Longville, a Gentleman of the Privy Chamber, and her marriage settlement allowed Custance to rebuild his house and empark and plant up 300 acres of heath.[126] To maintain the tangle of close connections, Thomas's younger brother George later married Mary's sister Charlotte Palmer, and settled near Thetford. The earliest image found showing Langley Hall when Sir Thomas was the owner is from Armstrong's *Histories and Antiquities of the County of Norfolk* and gives an idea of its appearance before its late eighteenth-century alterations (Figure 61).

Figure 61.
Engraving by I. Page of M. J. Armstrong's drawing of Langley in 1781 and published in his The History and Antiquities of the County of Norfolk, Vol. VII.

Some details of the life led by Thomas and Mary are captured in letters written by Mary to Edward Jerningham of Costessey between 1778 and 1812, a neighbour in London as well as in Norfolk. Writing to him from Langley she describes climbing onto the roof to catch a sunrise at 3.30 a.m., a place she calls 'a sacred spot'.[127] In January 1783 she confides to Edward how much she loves the place

> with all my little endearments . . . my children, my books, my morning and evening rides and walks, my solitary room (which I have completed to my wishes), my music, in short all but my husband I have here [he had gone to stay at Holkham, which she had side-stepped].[128]

She describes the park as 'a perfect paradise' for walking and riding, probably indicating that work had been done to provide the pleasant rides and drives proposed by Brown:

> I usually rise at seven, and take an hour's ride on horseback with the children upon the very horse which Sir Thomas offered you and which you begged I would use. It is the best and gentlest

creature imaginable; otherwise I should not chuse [*sic*] to ride him at this time.[129]

Sir Thomas continued his father's work both on the house and in the park. J. P. Neale described in c.1820 how the house had been given a wide porch with Doric pillars, and that the exterior was in '*brick, but coloured to represent stone*', which accounts for the creamy shade in which prints of the house appear at this time, made from a drawing by John Sell Cotman[130] (Figures 62 and 63).

Figure 62.
Ink and wash drawing by John Sell Cotman c.1810 showing the hall's new front porch. (Courtesy of Norfolk Museum Service: Norwich Castle Museum & Art Gallery)

Figure 63.
Hawksworth's engraving (from Cotman's drawing) showing Langley Hall with its rendered and white painted guise. (Private collection)

But Sir Thomas also made significant change to the landscape. He consulted Sir John Soane between 1784 and 1790 regarding designs for lodges and other possible ornaments for the park. These included a bathhouse for his thrice-weekly ablutions (Mary put his good health down to regular baths, while she couldn't abide bathing in any form[131]) as well as two designs for a rustic cottage, a hunting lodge, and three plans for entrance lodges. There was also a plan and section for a new roof for the main house.[132] The Chedgrave lodge (Figure 64) built around 1790, includes an imposing arch and a room each side, Coade stone greyhounds and the family motto featuring on the pediment. The Thurton lodge (Figure 65), adroitly placed at the lowest part of the park, accentuating the rise towards the house, is on a much smaller scale, taking elements such as arched windows and plain Doric pillars from Soane's drawings. The Carleton lodge (Figure 66) was added a century later and is in the form of a single rustic cottage.

Figure 64.
Soane's design for Chedgrave Lodge was completed in 1790 with chimneys concealed inside the arch. (Photo: Marcia Fenwick, 2016)

Figure 65.
Thurton Lodge and railings were completed in 1786. (Photo: Marcia Fenwick, 2016)

Figure 66.
Carleton Lodge built in the late nineteenth-century by Sir Reginal Proctor-Beauchamp.
(Photo: Marcia Fenwick, 2016)

It would appear that the north park remained enclosed for deer up until the time that the lodges were built. Langley's deer park was mentioned by Lord Hardwicke of Wimpole when advising one the King's stewards on an outbreak of deer disease at Windsor. He remarks that Sir Thomas successfully dealt with this problem at Langley in the 1770s by grazing geese that ate the rich grass or injurious weeds blamed for provoking the disease.[133] Oddly, Edward Jerningham preserved a note from Sir Thomas to him in 1789 accompanying a half buck carcass from Langley, with instructions for its dressing, adding, 'I desire, if you have wish for any more at any time, either for yourself or for your friends, that you will apply to me for it.'[134] However, when Edward asks Mary for some venison more than twenty years later, she responds from Lowestoft, (whilst accompanying her husband on a bathing holiday) with the reminder that 'we have disparked nearly twenty years', that is, they had given up the deer park around 1794–5.[135]

The changes made by Sir Thomas to his landscape are recorded in an estate map of Langley Park drawn up in 1816 [136] (Figure 67). The lodges and their drives are clearly shown and the lower park had been cleared of the double avenue. Broom Farm and its buildings are screened within a clump of conifers. This map, and Faden's county map of 1797, both show that the park extended over some 170 acres (70 hectares), its southern boundary still remaining along the line of the east–west thoroughfare shown on the map of c.1738, although this had been closed a while – presumably before 1771 – as there is no record of its closure in the Road Orders deposited in the Norfolk Record Office. The area to the south of this line had long been under arable cultivation and continued to be so even though it was enclosed within the shelter belt, planted against the road from Norwich to Chedgrave, and was included within the area shaded as 'park' on Faden's 1797 map. Long drives ran south/south-west and south-east from the hall, first through the grass park and then through the arable fields, to the new lodges designed by Soane.

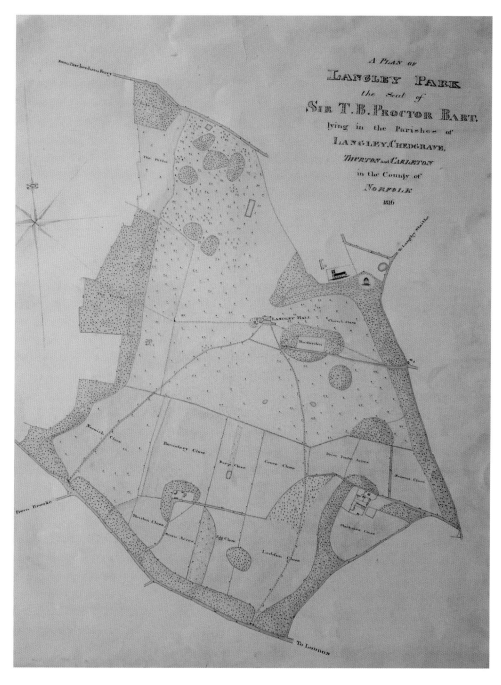

Figure 67.
1816 Estate Plan of Langley Park. (Norfolk Record Office: DS 157. Photo: Sally Bate 2016)

The 1816 map, and to an extent Faden's county map, allow us to assess the extent to which Brown's proposals for Langley, restricted to the northern section of the park, had been undertaken. They show that the most important of the changes proposed by Brown – the removal of Langley Wood and its incorporation within the area of the park – had indeed been carried out. Trees and underwood had been drastically thinned in the manner suggested by Brown, and the wood's western edge, and eastern end, retained as perimeter belts. As on Brown's plan, moreover, the long north boundary of the park, between these two areas of woodland, was left without a belt. In the north-west of the park six clumps, also formed by retaining parts of the wood, are clearly shown, although they rather differ in size and location to those originally proposed. The overall scheme for bringing Langley Wood within the park thus seems to have been adopted. Unlike the 1816 survey, the 1886 First Edition Ordnance Survey 25-inch to the mile plan shows the position of individual parkland trees. This indicates very clearly that, as Brown proposed, the timber was retained wholesale, leaving this north-western area of the park much more densely wooded than the rest. The 1886 OS map still marks the area occupied by the six clumps on the 1816 estate map as 'The Clumps', although they had now been absorbed into a wider area of woodland by subsequent planting (Figures 68 and 69).

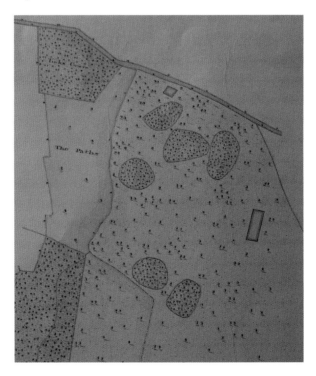

Figure 68.
Detail from the 1816 Estate Plan of Langley showing the six clumps of trees in the north of the park and the rectangular pond.

90

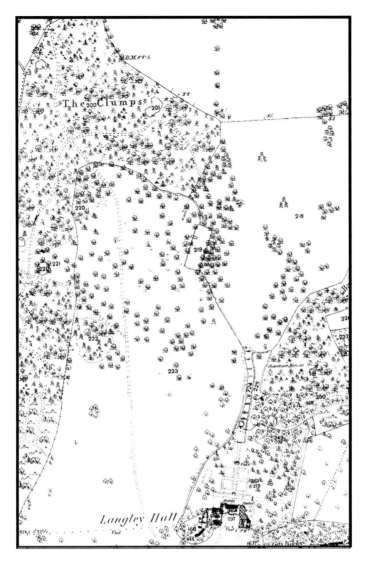

Figure 69.
1886 plan of Langley showing how the earlier Brownian clumps became amalgamated into the wooded belt, but the name persisted. (Reproduced from the Ordnance Survey 25-inch First Edition 1886 plan with kind permission of the Ordnance Survey)

The 1816 map also clearly shows the belts which Brown proposed to screen the kitchen garden, and those along the eastern and north-eastern margins of the park. They were wider belts of trees than he had recommended, and that on the park's eastern margins they were continuous rather than broken, although all are immediately recognisable.

91

Figure 70.
Lithograph of J.B. Ladbrooke's drawing of the pleasure ground at Langley in 1821. (Private collection. Photo: Marcia Fenwick, 2016)

Some aspects of Brown's plan do not seem to have been adopted; or if they were, they were soon altered. The sweeping ha-ha intended to enclose a spacious pleasure ground to the north of the house appears not to have been built. It is not indicated on Ladbrooke's lithograph dated 1821 (Figure 70). Moreover, the plan to create two large, lung-shaped clumps out of the old wildernesses to the north of the house does not seem to have been carried out either. The western of these two clumps appears to have been removed, while that to the east was partly removed and partly linked by additional planting to the north-eastern belt lying against the Chedgrave road. Within this belt, close to Grange Farm, the 1816 map shows a rotunda in a clearing in the trees, a stopping-off point on a tour round the park (Figure 71): a very 'Brownian' feature, although not shown on Brown's plan.

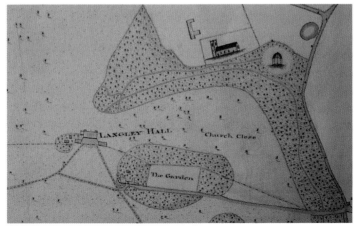

Figure 71.
Detail from the 1816 Estate Plan of the area around the hall, kitchen garden and tree belt south of the church.

More importantly, the lake proposed by Brown does not seem to have been created. Indeed, it is very hard to see how it *could* have been. There is no watercourse to dam here, and no obvious valley to fill with water, for most of the park occupies a low plateau. While it is true that the dryness of the land today perhaps belies the amount of water present in the past, a lake could only have been created by excavating a depression and filling it with water from springs or field ditches. All of Brown's other lakes were formed in whole or part by ponding back water along the valley of a stream, or river; there do not appear to be other examples of places where a lake was entirely created by excavation.

A possible answer to this puzzle may lie in the fact that, when Brown saw the landscape here, this area was entirely occupied by the mass of Langley Wood, making it hard to see the precise character of the natural land forms (the wood would have been coppiced, and thus quite densely filled with vegetation). Brown may have misjudged the character of the topography for this reason. Whatever the explanation, there is no evidence that a lake was even attempted here. It is true that the Tithe Award Map, surveyed in 1840, shows a rectangular pond in the approximate area of the suggested lake, but this is also shown by Brown in dotted lines just above the letter G on his plan and therefore pre-dates 1765 (Figure 57). This pond still exists. Another clue to the failure to create anything as large as Brown's proposed lake is clear from the evidence of the Ordnance Survey 6-inch First Edition, the earliest map to provide a clear indication of the pattern of trees within the park: for this shows Langley Wood's densely packed timber having no gap indicating the former presence of a large body of water.

The later history of Langley

Sir Thomas died at Langley in 1827. His widow Mary lived on into her ninetieth year, and one of their daughters, Amelia, married the third son of Sir Wodehouse of Kimberley, the Revd Hon. Armine Wodehouse, rector of West Lexham. Connections at various levels, social, political and familial, between the families over three generations may explain why it was not pure chance that the Beauchamp-Proctors and the Wodehouses used both Sanderson and Brown in making their 'improvements'.

The third baronet, a second Sir William, succeeded in 1827, by that time an admiral on the retired list. Sir William carried out some modifications to the house, commissioning Anthony Salvin (1799–1881) around 1828–30 to rebuild the two pavilions. A pair of sphinxes appear on the flanking walls, perhaps a memento of William's participation in the Egyptian campaign of 1801. The pavilions were reformed from seven bays wide into four, with larger windows. The creation of a splendid double-height ballroom in the east pavilion, with a billiard room and anteroom, which, together with the library, made an impressive entertaining suite. The Beauchamp-Proctor penchant for exuberant plasterwork ornament was allowed further expression in the coved ceiling for the ballroom, decorated in a Victorian interpretation of the Georgian style.

Sir William did not neglect the park, and a detailed account of its state and management was made by the dendrophile James Grigor in his *Eastern Arboretum* of 1841. Turning into the park off the Norwich road, Grigor was immediately struck by the miniature scale of the Thurton lodges, though their setting on open sward, framed by clumps of oak and beech, was attractive. Disappointed that the drive took him not into a wide vista dotted with deer or sheep but through the arable fields of the lower park, 'the farming premises, which are but partially obscured by a meagre belt, enhance the incongruity', his mood lifted when passing through the second gate, marking 'the proper commencement of the park'.[137] Here the former woodland had been cleared around 'noble trees', although Grigor felt more could have been done to increase the depth and breadth of the vistas. But he delighted in an under-planting of thorns round the clumps 'which afford, in an early season in particular, that green freshness which is truly delightful'. In front of the house two ancient Scotch pines make a striking feature on the open lawn, 'so wild and matted' he thought they were cedars of Lebanon, and he measured a 'noble oak' with a 14-foot girth. Behind the house, in a formal garden 'of no great size', there were clumps of evergreens on the lawns, but again 'the arable land runs in by far too closely to the house and parterre without even a semblance of a belt or screen to exclude it'. However, despite the modesty of the park and the imperfections noted, Grigor concluded:

> There are few places in the county which evince so decidedly that the hand of improvement is ever busy; while the careless profusion of wide-spreading oaks, which display themselves in every field around, give an air of dignity to the entire domain, and stamp it as one of prime importance in the district. [138]

Sir Thomas William Brograve Proctor-Beauchamp (1815–1874) succeeded as 4th baronet in March 1861. Brograve was the maiden name of his mother, the heiress of an estate near Chelmsford. Sir Thomas was responsible for switching the surname order. This enabled him to retain the Proctor element after the third generation, at which time a name gained by testamentary injunction is usually dropped. At any rate, the name appears only to have been used by the heads of the family, other members tending to use just 'Beauchamp'. Sir Thomas carried out a number of exterior works, focusing on the pleasure grounds on the north side of the house rather than the park.

Here he created a long, narrow lake suggesting the width of a river, running north and centred on the north–south axis of the house (Figure 72). At the southern end

Figure 72.
Victorian photograph of 19th-century lake looking north. (Langley School Archives)

he built a semi-circular terrace of white bricks, with steps leading down to the water, and between the terrace and the house a substantial pool containing a stone fountain, was set among geometric beds for colourful planting schemes. The spoil from digging the lake was piled in random heaps on its east side. One mound had a flint ruin built on it, and for added incongruity a thatched cottage close beside it, used as a teahouse (Figure 73).

Figure 73.
Victorian photograph of the 19th-century thatched teahouse and 'ruin' in the arboretum, positioned on the lake's east bank. (Langley School Archives)

Another mound concealed an ice house, the entrance of which is still visible although now permanently closed. The area to the west, which became known as the arboretum, displayed a range of ornamental trees, including holm oak, cedar and weeping beech, Corsican, Bhutan and Scots pine, and clumps of monkey-puzzle, deodar and Wellingtonia. Splendid eighteenth-century sweet chestnuts, originally planted within Langley Wood, gave height and substance to the new plantings and have survived to the present day.

Figure 74.
Edwardian photograph of the exterior of conservatory built by Woods of Chelsea. (Langley School Archives)

Sir Thomas commissioned Woods of Chelsea to design and build a substantial conservatory off the east front, adding a novel dimension to the reception suite (Figure 74). The elaborate structure, built in about 1865, complemented the curving corridor behind, with lofty gables, stained glass and a glass dome. It was heated by gas made on site near the exotic plant house and new forcing houses (50 feet long), also designed by Woods and installed between the house and the kitchen garden. The conservatory was only demolished in the 1950s, its brick base left to form a low wall. The impressive rear wall sculptures and a grotto from the winter garden remains a feature against the east wall of the house (Figure 75).

Sir Reginald Proctor-Beauchamp was the last baronet to leave his mark on the park. After succeeding in 1874 he moved a fifteenth-century cross, with four saints supporting the slender shaft, from near Langley Abbey to a position on the west side of the park, where it still stands, marking the meeting point of four parish boundaries.[139] Under Sir Reginald the park reached its greatest size, 803 acres, mainly through additional tree-planting schemes. Other works included renovation of the church and modernising the house, renewing the front porch and panelling the entrance hall in pollard oak, as well as installing plate glass in the windows and a clock on the front pediment.

Figure 75.
Part of the rear internal wall of the conservatory, now open to the elements since the structure was dismantled in the 1950s. (Photo: Roger Last, 2015)

After his death Sir Reginald left Langley to his eldest daughter Sheila (her uncles, in turn, gained the title but lived elsewhere) and she presided over Langley's last years as the home of the Beauchamps. She had a brief marriage to Major Herman Barker-Hahlo, and a *Country Life* article on Langley Park written by Oliver Brackett in 1927 describes it firmly as 'the seat of Mrs Barker-Hahlo' where she 'dispenses hospitality' at weekend parties.[140] Brackett noted that the stucco on the outside was now mostly falling off, revealing the original soft red brick below.

Sheila had caused a swimming pool to be cut out of the near end of the garden lake, and the gardens to the front and back made brilliant by scarlet bedding patterns. In 1939 Langley was requisitioned by the 4th Battalion of the Norfolk Regiment and was therefore not available to the 8th Baronet Dr Sir Ivor Proctor-Beauchamp when he returned from Szechuan, where he had been a missionary doctor.

After wartime use the Trustees of the Proctor-Beauchamps disposed of some of the art collection and larger pieces of furniture. In 1947 the Norwich High School for Boys took a lease of the house and grounds, and ten years later bought it. The remaining parkland was purchased by the Hutton family, who first built a house at Langley Grange, then converted Broom Farm. The parkland and some of the perimeter belt was clear-felled in the 1950s and the Chedgrave drive was ploughed up. New plantations, mainly of conifer and sycamore, have replaced much of the deciduous woodland. Many of the outbuildings have been converted or replaced by classrooms. Modern staff accommodation stands among what is left of the belt of trees (decimated in the 1987 storm) that Brown proposed around the kitchen garden and former orchard (Figure 76). The south wall of the kitchen garden blew down in the 1960s and has not been re-erected, but the other walls have been patched up in a variety of bricks and styles, and new buildings fill most of the original enclosure. The school continues to do much to preserve the interiors of the main house and outside the lake has been dredged and some of the Victorian bedding patterns round the fountain reinstated.

Figure 76.
Aerial photograph from the 1960s showing the Victorian arboretum in the north garden and a new building, extreme right. (Langley School Archives)

Although topographical and documentary evidence, as outlined in this chapter, indicate that the Beauchamp-Proctor family implemented the forestry elements of Brown's proposals, his 'intended water feature' and innovative curved ha-ha were conceptions that were perhaps too ambitious, especially as Sir William overspent on electioneering. With regard to the pleasure ground, it is hard to evaluate how much of Brown's ideas for the two large clumps were carried out, though the original wilderness was reworked at various stages. A few mature native species remain in the arboretum but the area is dominated by the Victorian lake and planting scheme. Planting following Brown's plan may be perceived in two specimen trees to the north of the house: a magnificent cedar, with a girth of 9.3 metres (30 feet), stands at the west end of the terrace and a lime with a girth of 5.3 metres (17 feet) marks the western boundary of the original pleasure grounds. Some half a dozen trees of Brownian vintage remain in the area south of the hall, all oaks with girths of around 4 metres (13 feet), whilst a clump of sweet chestnuts of mid-eighteenth-century size stand by the drive west of the house as he envisaged.

However, from the testimony of those who described the park it is clear that Brown's suggested plan had an enduring influence on its overall development. The family's lasting respect for him ensured that tree-planting was for several generations an absorbing interest, and that his original 1765 plan was carefully preserved.

The east drive avenue is partially replanted, but the most indicative element of Brown's design for Langley's park may be discerned in its perimeter plantings. While the north-western section of the park is now purely arable, the eastern and western ends of the woodland, seen by Brown as anchoring the peripheral belts, have been replanted and extended, using ash, sycamore and conifer. From both the Norwich Road and from within, the woods of Langley show a recognisably Brownian structure, with their rides and glades. The names of the various plantations – such as The Clumps and The Views – resonate with Brownian terminology.

CHAPTER 4 MELTON CONSTABLE

Melton Constable Park (Photo: ©Mike Page Aerial Photography)

Introduction

Melton Constable Park lies in a quiet part of North Norfolk, a little inland from the popular coastal settlements and tourist destinations. It was the home of the Astley family for over 700 years, and the hall and deer park today exhibit a timeless quality, and remain in private hands. In the past influential residents have made their mark nationally whether in government service, in military campaigns, or through contributions to the arts or even horse racing. However, most people who have heard of Melton Constable Hall remember it for being the home of the Maudsley family in the acclaimed 1971 film of L. P. Hartley's novel *The Go-Between*. The village of Melton Constable is unique in north Norfolk, as it developed rapidly between 1880 and the early 1900s when it became a railway junction for the new lines across East Anglia. Specifically designed artisan dwelling houses and community buildings grew up around the station and workshops[141] and the village expanded eastwards along the B1354 until it merged with the older settlement of Briston.

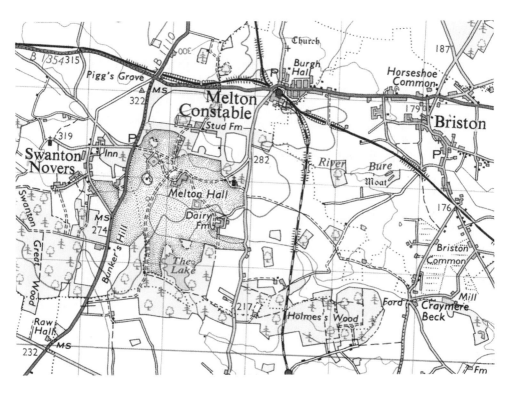

Figure 77.
Location map Melton Constable Park - OS. (Reproduced from the Ordnance Survey 1-inch 7th Series 1955-61 map with kind permission of the Ordnance Survey)

The parish of Melton Constable occupies an elevated position (for Norfolk) rising to 322 feet (98 metres) above sea level, the land dipping down towards the coastal communities of Blakeney and Cley, 8 miles (12.5 kilometres) to the north. White chalk underlies the clay soils, which contain pockets of glacial sand and gravel. The parish straddles a watershed; in the north, small streams run to the coast while within Melton Constable Park itself the river Bure rises and flows south-east through the northern Broads to Great Yarmouth. This whole area, including the park, was rather flat and poorly drained in the past, containing a high concentration of commons. It is still remarkably well wooded. When Lancelot Brown visited here in the 1760s, he would have undoubtedly been dismayed by the marshy terrain and the lack of natural contours to work with.

102

Melton Constable before 1764

Although there is archaeological evidence of pre-conquest settlement in the area, the oldest surviving building in Melton Constable is St Peter's Church, consecrated in 1092. It is a good example of a Late Saxon or Early Norman design with a central tower (Figure 78). South of the church, cropmarks shown on aerial photographs appear to indicate the site of a deserted settlement.[142]

Figure 78.
St Peter's Church, Melton Constable. (Photo: Roger Last, 2013)

The Manor of Melton or *Mealton* was granted to William de Beaufo, the Bishop of Thetford at the time of the Norman Conquest, and held by Roger de Lyons. De Lyons' descendants assumed the name Mealton and subsequently occupied the position of Constable under the bishop, signing themselves 'Melton de Constable' and so creating the name of the estate, and parish, which has continued until this day.[143] Domesday Book, compiled in 1086, describes *Mealton* as having 4 freemen, 2 villagers and 32 smallholders – a sizeable settlement for this period. In 1236 Sir Thomas de Astley (alias Estley) of Warwickshire married Editha, heiress of Peter le Constable of Melton, and for the next 700 years the Melton Constable estate remained in the hands of the Astley family. Other branches of this family held estates at Hillmorton in Warwickshire and Reading in Berkshire. Sir Thomas Astley was killed at the Battle of Evesham in 1265 and the estate passed to his five-year-old son Ralph. During his 82-year ownership Ralph Astley gained a charter from Edward I to enclose a deer park in 1290. The boundaries of deer parks normally consisted of a bank topped by a wooden pale (in other parts of the country the bank may be substituted with stone walls and in later parks with a brick wall). On the inside of this bank there would be a steep-sided ditch to prevent the deer escaping. At intervals, a rampart of earth or a *deer leap* on the outside might allow roaming deer to enter the park and then find they had no means of escape.[144] Ralph Astley created his deer park from an existing area of woodland and pasture and it is said that it was the second in England to be stocked with red deer.[145] This medieval deer park probably, although by no means certainly, developed into the park which existed here by the seventeenth century, and which itself developed into the great landscape designed by Brown.

The location of the Astley's medieval manor house, 370 metres (1,213 feet) south-east of the current hall, can still be seen today. The moated site, covering just over an acre, is said to contain the building's foundations but little is known about its form or construction.[146] Notable members of the family from this time include a second Ralph Astley (1321–1370) who fought in the Battle of Crecy (1346), Thomas Astley (b. 1383) who served Henry V and John Astley (1414–1475) who supported the Lancastrians in the Wars of the Roses.[147]

In 1496 Thomas Astley (1469–1543) inherited the estate and by the end of the century had built a new winged brick house, with service buildings around a central court, on higher ground to the north-west of the old moated site.[148] No known illustrations of the complete building survive but an estate map of 1674 (Figures 79 and 80) shows that, by this date, all that remained of the Tudor mansion was a single pile, symmetrical seven-bay house aligned north to south, with five chimney stacks and a roof with shaped gables. There is a suggestion that the house had fallen into disrepair during the Civil War. A small building is shown on the map, immediately to the south of the house, and this can be seen on later engravings as an octagonal banqueting house or viewing tower. On the east side of the adjoining fenced or walled court are two smaller service buildings along with a third to the north, all with pitched roofs and chimneys. The map shows that the court was subdivided by a wall or hedge, the southern part perhaps containing a private garden for family use. The house looked out westwards towards an L-shaped canal, beyond which was a complex of four geometric fish ponds. The park itself is shown as evenly planted with trees, and with a gabled building, perhaps a keeper's house or lodge. A second wooded area named 'The Park' can be seen to the east, which today forms part of Holme's Wood.

Thomas Astley married twice and had sons called John by both wives. His first son John (1504–1558) by Anne Broughton went on to inherit Melton Constable. His second wife was Anne Wood of East Barsham. Anne's sister had married Sir James Boleyn of Blickling (uncle of Anne Boleyn) and as a result Thomas Astley had influential friends at Henry VIII's court. Thomas's second son named John and his wife, Catherine Campernown, held positions in Princess Elizabeth's household,

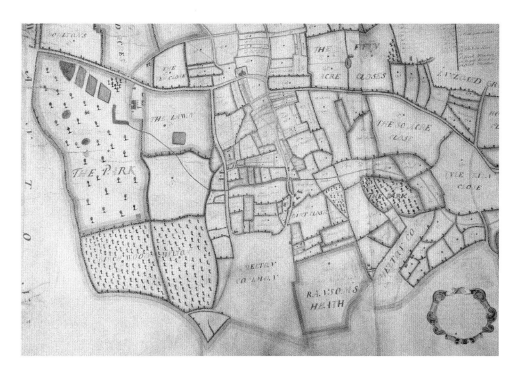

Figure 79.
Estate map of Melton Constable, 1674, redrawn by Thomas Becket in 1732. (Norfolk Record Office: HAY 82/83, photo: Roger Last, 2016)

Figure 80.
Detail of the 1674 estate map, showing the deer park, fish ponds, Tudor house and service yard.

105

and Catherine was with the Princess at the time of her mother's execution. During Mary's reign John fled to France for safety but after his return, Elizabeth trusted him enough to appoint him as her Master of the Jewel House in 1558.[149]

The estate passed from John Astley to Isaac Astley (1540–1598), who married Mary Waldegrave of Lawford in Essex. This marriage produced no less than 16 children and the estate passed down from the eldest son Thomas (1567–1617) to two of his sons, Sir Francis and Sir Isaac. As both died without a male heir, in 1659 Melton Constable was inherited by their nephew Jacob, whose father Edward (1604–1654) had married his cousin Elizabeth Astley. Elizabeth was the daughter of Sir Jacob Astley, created Baron of Reading after fighting for the king at Naseby, Newbury and Gloucester. As was common during the Civil War, Elizabeth was caught between both sides, her husband Edward and his elder brother Sir Isaac – owner of Melton Constable – siding with the Parliamentarian forces, whilst her father Jacob and two brothers were Royalists.[150] R. W. Ketton-Cremer published a collection of touching letters sent from Edward to his wife while she was living at Bale, and later Hindolveston, in which he often makes reference to 'little Jacob' his son. After the siege of Oxford old Sir Jacob Astley was imprisoned in Warwick Castle before finally, in 1646, being allowed to come home to live in Hindolveston with his daughter Elizabeth, Parliamentarian son-in-law Edward and grandson Jacob, later Sir Jacob Astley (1639–1729).[151]

Figure 81.
Sir Jacob Astley 1st Baronet, who inherited Melton Constable in 1659 and commissioned the 'Wren-style' house completed in 1687. This 1660–5 portrait by Gerard Soest can be seen at NT Seaton Delaval Hall. (©National Trust Images)

It was the younger of these two Jacob Astleys who commissioned the building of the present Melton Constable Hall, which was finished shortly after 1687. Charles II made Sir Jacob 1st Baronet Astley of Hillmorton in 1660 and he married Blanch Wodehouse, of Kimberley Park, in 1661. He was High Sheriff of Norfolk in 1664 and represented Norfolk as a MP from 1695 to 1701, 1702 to 1705 and again from 1710 to 1722.[152]

Sir Jacob almost certainly would have known, or known of, Sir Christopher Wren and although neither the name of the architect, nor plans, for the 1680s house appear to survive, Melton Constable Hall has been described as an important and rare survival of a 'Wren Style House' outside the environs of London. It was built of red brick, relatively modest in size, rectangular, of nine bays by seven, all under a hipped roof crowned by a cupola, later removed.[153] Norfolk Museums' Service has in its collection a scale architect's model of Sir Jacob's new building (Figure 82) and a glimpse of the newly completed house also appears in the background of a lavish portrait of Sir Jacob's youngest son, John Astley (Figure 83).

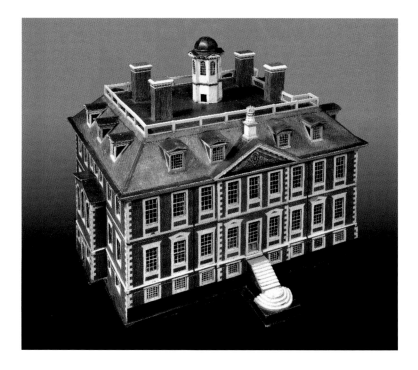

Figure 82.
Scale architect's model of Melton Constable. (Norfolk Museums' Service (Gressenhall Farm and Workhouse NWHCM: 1971.386)

Figure 83.
Portrait of John Astley (youngest son of Sir Jacob 1st Bt) by John Closterman. We know this was painted in 1690 and John was aged 13, as this is painted on the bottom of the plinth, and in the background is the family's new house. (Courtesy of NT Seaton Delaval Hall and ©National Trust Images/John Hammond)

Various individuals have been suggested as the architect of the hall, including Hugh May, whose Eltham Lodge closely resembles Melton Constable; Roger Pratt, who had travelled Europe to study Renaissance architecture and who had Norfolk connections, designing his own house, Ryston Hall, in 1669; and William Samwell, who built the new addition at Felbrigg Hall in 1674. Certainly the stucco work at Melton Constable appears to be by the same artist as was employed by Samwell at Felbrigg.[154]

The earliest complete image of Sir Jacob's new hall is that published by Kip and Knyff in their *Britannia Illustrata* of 1707 (Figure 84); it was the only property in Norfolk they considered worth including in their book. In the 34 years which had elapsed since the 1674 estate map was surveyed, the Melton Constable landscape had undergone huge changes. Several new, walled courts had been laid out, elaborately planted with parterres and topiary, the largest of which, south of the new hall, contained a canal stretching towards a double tree-lined avenue which continued to the southern boundary of the park. This alignment, and indeed the whole extensive design, was centred on the axis of the symmetrical building, with its four chimney stacks around the central lantern and cupola. Further avenues of trees extended at right-angles, east and west. The western avenue led to a square building with a three-storey tower at the front. This still exists today and is now known by its nineteenth-century title, the 'Bath House'.[155] It was probably built as a 'standing' or hunting tower overlooking the deer park and the thickness of the walls suggests that the ground floor could have served as a game larder. This building does not look much like the feature shown occupying the same site on the 1674 map – the putative keeper's lodge, noted above – but there are doubts about the accuracy of the latter source in this regard and certainly, the style and construction of the building, and especially the shape of the fireplace on the first floor, suggest late sixteenth- or seventeenth-century origins.[156] Kip and Knyff show numerous deer grazing within what is evidently a much enlarged park, the high walls of the garden enclosures preventing them from straying into the parterres and flower beds; the park would have been enclosed by a pale more than 4 miles (6.5 kilometres) long to prevent them escaping.

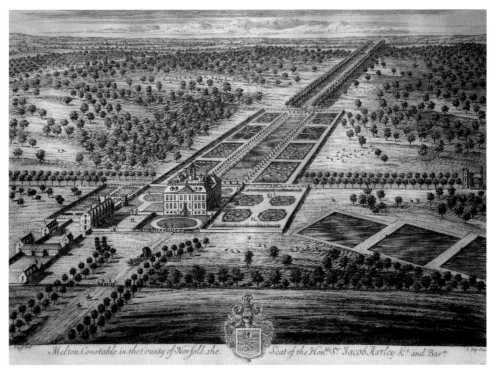

Figure 84.
Jan Kip and Leonard Knyff's 1707 engraving of Melton Constable Park from their book 'Britannia Illustrata', showing the elaborate formal gardens, canal and avenues of trees. (S. P. Fenny, photo: Roger Last 2016)

The remaining wing of the Tudor house had been retained by Sir Jacob as a service building with servant accommodation above. Still evident near its southern end is the octagonal banqueting house, and also retained were the two pitched roofed buildings (extreme left) from the 1674 map. These two structures, and the Tudor house itself, are still extant today although they have undergone much change. The medieval fish 'stews' or ponds to the north-east of the new hall had likewise survived, their banks apparently straightened and their water levels regulated by the use of sluice gates. David Yaxley has suggested that they may have also fed the ornamental canal in the garden by means of underground pipes.[157]

Certainly, Sir Jacob did not stint in the creation of his new home, gardens and park, following the fashions of the day. However, by the early 1730s the formal gardens had already begun to be dismantled. They were largely removed after Sir Jacob's death in 1729, under his son Sir Philip Astley 2nd Baronet (1667–1739) and then his grandson Sir Jacob Astley 3rd Baronet (1692–1760).

Figure 85.
Edmund Prideaux' 1735 sketch of Melton Constable Hall from the west. (From the collection of P. J. N. Prideaux-Brune, Prideaux Place, Padstow. Image: Historic England Archives: AA75/02222)

Figure 86.
Samuel and Nathaniel Bucks' 1741 engraving of the 'South West view of Melton Constable'. (© Crown copyright: UK Government Art Collection, AA75/02222)

A drawing made around 1735 by Edmund Prideaux (Figure 85) shows some of the walled courts remaining but the ornamental beds and avenues of trees appear to have gone. A 1741 illustration by Samuel and Nathaniel Buck shows the hall standing on a modest raised terrace or building platform amongst a much more open landscape (Figure 86). By this time, landscape architects such as Kent were already working in a much more 'informal' way, at places like Stowe in Buckinghamshire, and nearby Holkham in Norfolk. Such complicated parterres were not only becoming out of fashion, but also costly in their upkeep. The gardens shown on Kip and Knyff's engraving were thus short-lived, for fashions in garden design changed as rapidly in the past as they do today. Sir Jacob Astley 3rd Baronet (Figures 87 and 88) was a fervent supporter of the arts and himself an accomplished musician, composer and writer. He also liked planting trees.[158] The natural informality shown on Samuel and Nathaniel Buck's illustration would have appealed to his classical tastes.

Melton Constable Park passed to Jacob's son Sir Edward Astley, 4th Baronet (1729–1802), in 1760. In 1751 Sir Edward had married Rhoda Delaval (Figures 89 and 90), an artist and the eldest daughter of Captain Francis Blake Delaval of Seaton Delaval in Northumberland, although sadly the marriage was short-lived as

111

Figure 87.
Sir Jacob Astley 3rd Baronet, by John Theodore, the elder. (NT Seaton Delaval Hall and ©National Trust Images)

Figure 88.
Sir Jacob Astley 3rd Bt. with his family, including his son and heir, Sir Edward (standing with a dog on the right), painted in the 1730s and attributed to Petrus Johannes van Reysschoot. (Courtesy of NT Seaton Delaval Hall and ©National Trust Images/John Hammond)

Rhoda died in childbirth in 1757. Despite Rhoda having three brothers, two died without issue and the third did not have children who lived long enough to inherit the Seaton Delaval Estate, which therefore passed to Rhoda and Edward's son Jacob in 1814.[159] Sir Edward would marry twice more and have four children with his second wife Anne Milles. As was commonly the case when large estates and houses gained a new owner, Edward started to make major changes at Melton Constable. He was a politician (MP for Norfolk, holding the same seat as his Great Grandfather Sir Jacob, from 1768 until retiring in 1790) and had an interest in farming, breeding horses, planting, building and improving his estate, which he owned for 42 years. In particular, he had a fine collection of books and an inventory of 1799, listing his pictures, silver, furniture and extensive library, has survived.[160] His paintings included works by Canaletto, Teniers, Van Dyck and Velázquez; and in his library were many titles on gardening, planting, husbandry and natural history. So it is not too surprising that he called upon the leading man at the time, Lancelot 'Capability' Brown, to help him improve the landscaping at Melton Constable.

Figure 89.
Sir Edward Astley 4th Bt. by Francis Cotes RA, in 1769. (Courtesy of NT Seaton Delaval Hall and ©National Trust Images/John Hammond)

113

Figure 90.
Rhoda Delaval, Lady Astley, attributed to Francis Cotes RA (Courtesy of NT Seaton Delaval Hall and ©National Trust Images/John Hammond)

Lancelot Brown at Melton Constable

In 1764, the year in which he began work at Melton Constable for Sir Edward, Lancelot Brown was appointed Master Gardener to the gardens of Hampton Court, Richmond and St James. He moved into Wilderness House at Hampton Court with his wife Bridget and children, during a particularly busy time of his career.[161] Unfortunately, Brown's plan for the site – which he would have shown Sir Edward when outlining the changes he proposed to make – has not survived. However, as recently as 2013 the contract drawn up between the two men was deposited in the Norfolk Records Office, with other Astley papers from Seaton Delaval by the National Trust. Figure 91 shows a photograph of the contract and Figure 92 a transcript made by the Norfolk Gardens Trust Research Group.

Figure 91.
The original 1764 contract between Sir Edward Astley 4th Bt. and Lancelot Brown. (Norfolk Records Office: ACC2013/217, photo: Roger Last, 2016)

Contract between Lancelot Brown and Sir Edward Astley Bt for works at Melton Constable Hall
July 1764
Then an agreement made between Sir Edward Astley Bt on the one part, and Lancelot Brown on the other for the underwritten article of work to be performed at Milton [sic] Constable in the County of Norfolk (to wit) –

Article the 1st To make the large piece of water in the park, in all its parts, making a sufficient head putting in a proper plug and forming its edges etc. Making the whole water from 2ft and a half to 18ft in water.

Article the 2nd. To make all the necessary plantations which are intended in the park and garden.

Article the 3rd. To make all the roads within the park in width and direction as set out and agreed to, and to drain all the wet parts where the roads are to go through.

Article the 4th To make and plant all the intended kitchen and pleasure garden in all their parts, as also the sunken fence to enclose them, Sir Edward to be at all the expenses in walls and fence to the Pleasure Garden, the sinking of the ground excepted.

Article the 5th. To make the ground part of the Menagerie, planting the necessary trees and shrubs making the gravel walks.

Article the 6th. To drain all the wet parts within the plantations on the sides of the drives and to make the walk or drive quite through the Plantation.

Article the 7th. To level and adorn the ponds near the house with plantations etc. as agreed to by Sir Edward, as also the ground between the house and the pond, and that where the present kitchen garden stands, nursery and stews, giving the whole a naturally corresponding level with the park in general etc.

The said Lancelot Brown does promise for himself his heirs administrators and assigns to perform or cause to be performed in the best manner in his or their power the above written articles between the date thereof and June or July Seventeen sixty-eight.
For the due performance of the above articles the Said Sir Edward Astley Bt does promise for himself his heirs administrators and assigns to pay or cause to be paid to the said Lancelot Brown his heirs administrators or assigns the sum of two thousand two hundred and eighty pounds of lawful money of England at the underwritten times of payment.
Sir Edward Astley to find at his expense carts, wheelbarrows, six if it was but 4 able horses during the execution of the work as also trees and shrubs.
[In another hand] Mem. Brown is to sink the fence between Wood's farm house and the church.

Figure 92. *Transcript of page 1 and 2 of Sir Edward Astley and Lancelot Brown's 1764 contract. (Transcribed by Janet Ede, 2015)*

An early account of the results of Brown's work to improve Sir Edward's landscape can be found in Armstrong's 1781 *History and Antiquities of the County of Norfolk*. His description of Melton Constable reads:

> The park contains about six or seven hundred acres, and is four miles in circumference, paled round, and finely diversified with buildings, wood and water. The great canal has been very judiciously improved by the ingenious Mr Browne [*sic*], whose taste in the disposition of objects in the pleasure grounds is equal to any: we are, not withstanding, of the opinion that something more may be done to this fine villa. The temple, menagery [*sic*], Belle-view, church, stables, boat-house and porters lodge, are seen to advantage in different points of view as you approach the house from the south. In the menagery Lady Astley has a curious collection of birds.[162]

Brown's contract describes, under seven articles, the work to be carried out by his men between 1764 and the proposed completion date of June or July 1768. For his part, Sir Edward undertook to provide the carts and wheelbarrows required and at least four, but preferably six, able horses, as well as all the trees and shrubs for the scheme. Article 7 refers to the 'present kitchen garden, stands, nursery and stews' (ponds) so it seems likely that a lot of the plant material was propagated and grown on the estate. The document goes on to lay out the schedule of payments. This contract and Brown's own account books are testament that Sir Edward Astley (unlike many of Brown's clients) settled his bills.[163] In total, Sir Edward paid £2,280 in nine instalments and Brown signed the project off in October 1768. There is nothing in the contract that indicates Brown planned any buildings or altered the Bath House. It is said that Brown supplied drawings for a temple, an aviary and a gothic summer house,[164] and Dorothy Stroud[165] and Edwards Hyams[166] have described how he built a 'little gothic castle' by the lake. Armstrong's reference (above) to a boathouse is the earliest mention of a building by the lake until the appearance of a 'tea house' here in the early nineteenth century, but it is possible that a castle-like boathouse once existed by the water. Several sources[167] talk about the Bath House being ornamented or gothicised by Brown, in part because of its resemblance to structures he designed or altered at Wallington, Blenheim and Burghley.[168] The castellated building (Figure 93) appears to have formed part of Brown's menagerie, referred to in Article 5 of the contract, and its 'gothicisation' may have been included in the works scheduled here, without separate listing. It does look very like Brown's High Lodge at Blenheim, also built in the 1760s (Figure 94). Although the depictions of the Bath House by Kip and Knyff, Prideaux and Buck are rather sketchy and very small, none show windows with pointed arches. It would seem that even if Brown did not embellish the window openings himself, the gothic arches date from around his

Figure 93.
The Grade II* listed Bath House, Melton Constable Park in the 1980s. (Photo courtesy of Stephen Heywood at Norfolk County Council)

Figure 94.
High Lodge at Blenheim Park, Oxfordshire, built by Capability Brown c.1768. (Courtesy of the Blenheim Estate, 2014)

time. Two larger arched windows were inserted in the south-west elevation to give a fine view over the deer park towards the distant lake. Sometime in the nineteenth or twentieth century these were blocked up, but have been reinstated over the past five years as part of ongoing renovation works.

Comparison of the Brown contract in the Norfolk Record Office with Brown's accounts book kept at the Royal Horticultural Society's Lindley Library reveals that a further payment, of £207, was received from Sir Edward Astley in December 1769. This could have been for supplying plans for the buildings described by Stroud and other writers, or perhaps for making the alterations to the Bath House. It is possible that the 'temple' at Melton Constable referred to by various eighteenth-century writers, may in fact have been the Bath House. The detail from Watt's illustration (Figure 95) depicts it looking very like a building worthy of this title, although the artist has exaggerated its size, proportionate to that of the hall itself.

Figure 95.
Detail of Melton Constable's Bath House looking more like a temple on William Watt's engraving for 'Seats of the Nobility and Gentry' 1782. (For the full image see Figure 101)

The creation of Melton Constable's lake, as detailed in Article 1 of the contract, was by far the greatest change to be made to the landscape during the 1760s. Sir Edward will have been keen to emulate the many lakes created by his social peers but he did not own a piece of land with a natural valley and a respectable watercourse to dam. The work force and time needed to create the huge lake is not specified separately but the feature must have been very costly. Today, the lake covers an area of 6.3 hectares (15 square acres), has a length of nearly 0.5 km (over 540 yards) and is 270 metres (295 yards) at its widest. Without a plan dating from Brown's time it is hard to determine how much its original shape differs from that of today. The draft 2-inch Ordnance Survey drawings of 1816 (Figure 96) seem to show a much simpler design, with two rounded expanses of water, each containing a small island, and with a projecting strip of land almost separating them. The 1850 Tithe Map (Figure 97) and early OS maps (Figure 98), however, depict an irregular form much more like that of today. It is perhaps unlikely that Brown would have designed a lake like the one shown on the 1816 OS drawing, as the view from the hall would have been foreshortened along its length.

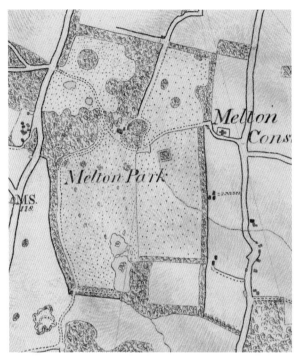

Figure 96.
Detail of Metcalf's 1816 survey drawing for the Ordnance Survey, of Melton Constable Park. (British Library: OSD 244 Fakenham Sheet 11)

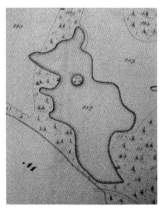

Figure 97.
Detail of the Melton Constable Tithe Map of 1850 showing Brown's lake. (Norfolk Records Office DNDA/978, photo: Roger Last, 2016)

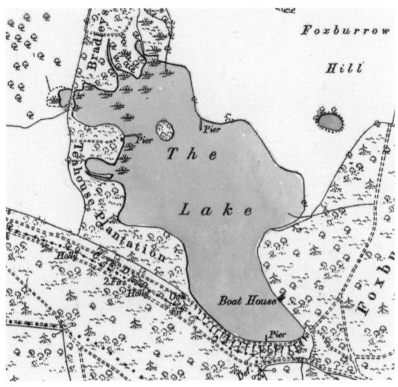

Figure 98.
Brown's lake at Melton Constable (Reproduced from the Ordnance Survey 1885 First Edition 6-inch to the mile map with kind permission of the Ordnance Survey)

Another difference between the lakes usually created by Brown, and that designed at Melton Constable, concerns its distance from the hall. Viewed from the main reception rooms Sir Edward and his guests would not have had an ideal view of his new 'piece of water', and by 1781 the lantern atop the building, which would have provided the best vantage point, had been taken down. The earliest illustration showing the lake is the sketch made by Humphry Repton for Armstrong's *History and Antiquities of the County of Norfolk* of 1781 (Figure 99), and in which the author writes 'from the top (of the house) there is an extensive prospect to the east, south and west; there is a staircase and door to the roof, which is of lead and flat'.[169] Repton has used a fair amount of artistic licence in his portrayal and brought the lake much closer than the 830 metres (just over 0.5 mile), which really separates the hall from the water's edge (Figure 100). The lake is too distant to be fed by the former fish ponds north-west of the hall, the land sloping too gradually to provide an adequate fall, so Brown made use of a small watercourse which ran across the southern section of the park. The *plug* in Article 1 refers to the sluice gate placed in the dam which he created at the east end of the lake, to allow the water to run off into the Blackwater Beck a little above its confluence with the upper Bure near Saxthorpe.

120

Figure 99.
Humphrey Repton's drawing of Melton Constable from the north-west which appeared in Armstrong's 1781 'The History and Antiquities of the County of Norfolk, Volume VII'.

Figure 100.
The distant view of Brown's lake from the south terrace at front of the hall, with later nineteenth-century balustrading and associated garden features in the foreground. (Photo: Sally Bate, 2015)

Melton Constable's lake, as depicted on nineteenth-century maps and as it exists today, bears little resemblance to most of the pieces of water which Brown designed for his clients. It is neither sinuous nor serpentine, but most irregular in shape and, according to Arthur Young writing in 1771, it was 'made with uncommon difficulty, which when properly united with wood will have a good effect'.[170] As a consequence of the flatness of the site and the lack of a convenient watercourse, it would seem that Sir Edward's lake functioned, at best, as a beguiling glimpse, designed to tempt visitors to ride out from the house and tour the grounds. Not only would the lake serve as a picturesque destination on the four-mile circuit of the park, but its banks would provide a location for painting, fishing, picnicking or, as suggested in Watt's engraving of 1782, an opportunity for boating (Figure 101).

Figure 101.
Watt's 1782 engraving of Melton Constable published in 'Seats of the Nobility and Gentry'.
(Private collection)

When Lancelot Brown first visited Melton Constable in 1764, he would have found, as we have noted, a landscape already largely cleared of geometric clutter and walled enclosures, and, to judge from Buck's engraving of 1741, with much planting of fairly young trees around the house. Within the park itself, where the 1674 map and Kip and Knyff's engraving both already show a considerable amount of tree planting, merging with Birch Wood to the south, Brown added belts of trees on the perimeter, whilst maintaining a drive through them for driving or riding, with occasional 'windows' in the planting to afford views across the lake, to the hall or church. A visitor in 1767 refers to the 'lately made' plantations 'which wind around the park, parallel with the pales'.[171] Brown would also have planted small groups of trees in the open parkland to arrest the eye or frame a feature. John Chambers, writing in 1829, reported that the park had been 'judiciously improved' and a 'fine piece of water now unites with the rich plantations, in rendering this spot one of the most perfect and pleasing in the county'.[172] Brown would almost certainly have removed or relocated trees that obstructed views from (or towards) the hall or hindered the effect of a planned vista within the park. The 1812 Ordnance Survey drawings show a solid belt of trees around the entire park boundary, effectively screening off any view into the landscape beyond and hiding all other buildings, including the church. Any trees planted in the 1760s in the deer park, and which survived until the twentieth century, were felled during the wide-scale clearances in the 1950s, including, it is reported locally, ancient oaks and yews. A 2015 tree survey by Norfolk Gardens Trust, in the vicinity of the hall, found a mere three yews, an oak and two limes (east of the kitchen garden), and a single yew by the Bath House, the size of which might conceivably indicate that they were planted at the time of Brown's activities at Melton Constable. The aerial photograph at the beginning of this chapter shows a partial avenue in the deer park, on the central axis of the hall, reminiscent of that shown by Kip and Knyff's illustration in 1707, but the trees here are comparatively young and the feature is a Victorian attempt to re-create part of the earlier formal setting for the hall, and would not have featured in Sir Edward's park.

Quite how many of the new 'roads' mentioned in the third article of Brown's contract were actually created, and which sections needed adequate drainage put in place, is not easy to ascertain. The 1674 estate map portrays a drive or track running north to south past the Tudor house, and another travelling at right angles from this, skirting the moated site and leading to a network of small fields. These must have been removed or rerouted before the extensive formal gardens, shown on Kip and Knyff's engraving of 1707, were laid out around the hall. Another road shown on the 1674 map, running west from St Peter's Church and passing close to the north side of the hall, before ending at a junction with what is now the B1110 (Guist to Thornage road), must have remained in place until the passing of a road closure order in 1784.[173] The term 'roads' used in the contract may lead the modern reader to imagine smartly surfaced thoroughfares open to all, when what Brown was actually asked to build were private drives around the park. He almost certainly designed the new drive, shown on Faden's county map of 1797, which sweeps in from the west gate to the front of the hall, over carefully levelled ground and the site of the former southern fish pond. The other 'roads' mentioned in the contract probably included routes for driving around the park (and through the perimeter belt), to enjoy views of the new landscape; and a secondary approach to the hall, running in from what was then the south-east park entrance. This route was described by both Armstrong in 1781(see above) and John Chambers in 1829, who noted how the grounds, park buildings and village church were seen to their greatest advantage when approaching the house from the south.[174] This drive would have passed over the marshy ground near the small springs feeding the lake, perhaps explaining the references to the need 'to drain all the wet parts where the roads are to go through', mentioned in article 3 of the contract.

The issue of drainage is addressed again in the sixth article of the contract. Situated at the sources of the Bure and Blackwater, the park contains numerous small springs and areas of boggy ground, and so Brown (a well-known drainage expert) was tasked with remedying this. In the main deer park no evidence has to date been uncovered of underground culverts, of the kind reported to exist at Kimberley, but nearer the house an entrance to one such drain survives in the area immediately to the south of the fish ponds. This could, however, be a relic of the water supply to the 1700s formal canal or, more likely, part of a nineteenth-century system supplying water to the south terrace fountains. Elsewhere, the clauses in the contract suggest that the existing woodland in the south of the park, and maybe elsewhere, needed improving by digging drainage channels, in order to create rides through the trees. A route through damp woodland suitable for carriage driving was a very different prospect to one for ridden horses. Flints and old bricks would have been laid as a sub-base, incorporating under-drains where necessary, before a top dressing of gravel was laid.

It has been suggested in the past that the kitchen garden at Melton Constable pre-dated Brown's activities.[175] If so, the reference in article 4 of the contract to 'making and planting the intended kitchen garden' was more of a renovation project. In fact, a survey undertaken by Norfolk Gardens Trust in 2015 proved that Brown did indeed build a new walled garden, albeit alongside the enclosure shown on the 1674 map and in Kip and Knyff's 1707 illustration. The north, east and south walls of the present garden evidently date from the 1760s. Only the western side is in part older, comprising the two small service buildings, which originally occupied the eastern side of the 1674 enclosure (a full explanation of these findings is provided elsewhere[176]).

The gap (shown as Section C on Figure 102) between these two older buildings was later infilled by a gardeners' or grooms' bothy. Careful inspection of the brickwork reveals, however, that this was originally a simple wall, laid in English bond, linking the two structures – the boundary shown on the 1674 map, with a small gateway at its centre. Similar brickwork is found in the stretch of wall south of the Tudor building (Section B), a wall which Brown extended further to the south – a feature again shown clearly on the 1674 map, and on Kip and Knyff's

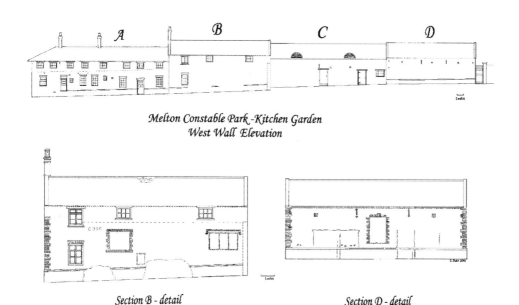

Melton Constable Park -Kitchen Garden
West Wall Elevation

Section B - detail   Section D - detail

Figure 102.
Elevation drawings of the buildings which comprise the western side of Brown's kitchen garden. Section A: 19th-century cottages built on to a 16th-century wall. Sections B and D: originally Tudor service buildings. Section C: 19th-century bothy built onto 16th-century wall. (Sally Bate, 2015)

Figure 103.
South-east corner of Brown's kitchen garden at Melton Constable. (Photo: Roger Last, 2015)

engraving. In the nineteenth century the cottages in Section A were built using the garden wall as part of their front elevation, the dotted line on Figure 102 indicating the change in brickwork. Brown's kitchen garden measured 134 by 52 metres (441 by 172 feet) and enclosed an area of 0.71 hectares (1.75 acres). The new 1760s walls were constructed of red brick laid in Flemish bond and were probably fired at the nearby Swanton Novers brick kilns (Figure 103). Due to the way that the land slopes significantly – at an angle of around 5 per cent – towards the east, the north wall (and a central dividing wall, erected later in the eighteenth century) have courses laid parallel to the ground. In the mid- to late nineteenth century the east, north and dividing wall were all were heightened in such a way that the tops became horizontal using a series of steps, presumably to accommodate the glasshouses erected along them. The walls were then capped with ornately shaped coping tiles (Figure 104).

Figure 104.
19th-century ornamental coping tiles – a later addition to Brown's walls in the kitchen garden. (Photo: Sally Bate, 2015)

The exact internal design of the garden and details of what was grown there in the eighteenth century are not known. Bryant's small-scale map of Norfolk, published in 1826, shows diagonal paths crossing in a saltire design; however, the accuracy of this map, as discussed below, is uncertain. The 1850 Tithe Map shows paths enclosing three square plots with further beds lining the base of the walls (Figure 105). The northernmost plots are separated by a long garden building, possibly a potting shed or glasshouse, which no longer exists. There are two pedestrian entrances, apart from those leading in from the stable yard, which are still in use today. The paths from these would take visitors around the newly established pleasure garden, which was wrapped around the outside of the walled garden and separated from the wider parkland by Brown's 'sunken fence' or ha-ha.

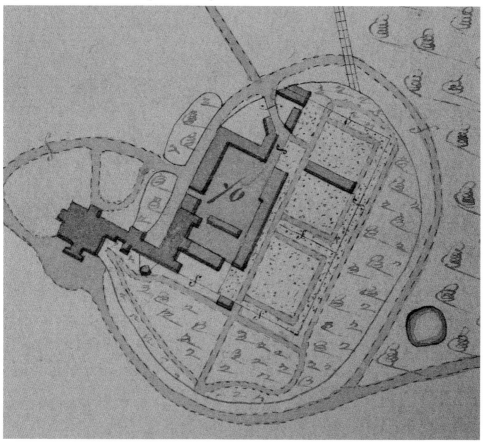

Figure 105.
Detail of the 1850 Tithe Map of Melton Constable showing the hall, service buildings, stable yard and kitchen garden surrounded by the pleasure garden within the ha-ha. (Norfolk Records Office DNDA/978, photo: Roger Last, 2016)

The term 'sunken fence' is ambiguous. Some of these features consisted of a line of palings, or a wall, running along the bottom of a sizeable ditch; others involved an asymmetrical ditch, the internal side formed by a vertical retaining wall. At Melton Constable, both would have needed to have been very substantial to exclude red deer. The present ha-ha enclosing the area of the pleasure ground is an asymmetrical ditch retained by a late eighteenth-century brick wall. Its original form is unknown, but perhaps comprised a free-standing fence in a ditch, a reasonably inexpensive design, considering all the timber available locally. The 1850 Tithe Map charts its route, starting at the south-east corner of the hall, and encircling the walled kitchen garden, with the intervening spaces forming the pleasure garden. A door in the eastern elevation of the hall provided access to the pleasure ground, and from thence to the kitchen garden, so that family and guests could undertake a short stroll amongst the flowers, ornamental shrubs and productive fruit and vegetable beds, which was, in effect, a miniature version of the longer circuit tour around the park. The Tithe Map shows the early octagonal banqueting house (as a small grey circle), indicating its survival as a feature of the pleasure grounds well into the nineteenth century, together with another small building built into the south side of the southern kitchen garden wall. This could have been a summer house, evidently added since the time of Brown, as two rebates have been cut into the kitchen garden wall, to house the upright posts which formed part of the building's structure. A large portion of the sunken fence or ha-ha survives today, although it no longer serves its original function. The stretch nearest the hall was, however, lost during the extensive remodelling of the gardens, and terrace-building, by the Victorian generations of the Astley family. The ha-ha's internal bank now has a retaining wall using slightly larger and more uniform bricks than those in the kitchen garden – probably late eighteenth-century in date – capped with large, terracotta coping tiles at its southern end and smaller terracotta tiles to the north (Figure 106). Despite the years of leaf litter accumulation, the depth of the ha-ha varies from 1.6 to 2 metres (5ft 2 in–2ft 6 in) in height and between 3.9 to 4.6 metres (12ft 9 in–15ft 1 in) in width. Another function of this feature would have been drainage and at one or two places the ends of drains and a culvert (both of unknown date) running from the pleasure garden can still be seen.

Figure 106.
Section of the late eighteenth-century ha-ha on the eastern side of the pleasure garden.
(Photo: Roger Last, 2015)

Sir Edward Astley paid Brown to create a site, behind the Bath House, for a new menagerie, complete with gravel paths for visitors to view the collection. The clause in the contract includes the words, 'planting the necessary trees and shrubs', which may refer to planting inside the menagerie but probably refers to the large block of trees established to the north and west, shown on the 1816 Ordnance Survey drawing. The menagerie, fronted by the Bath House, would have fitted seamlessly into the natural landscaping, and provided a noteworthy stopping point on the tour round the park. As Figure 107 shows, there is a large section (74 metres/81 yards) of wall, apparently of eighteenth-century date, still standing here, which would have enclosed the menagerie. This wall differs in construction from those around the kitchen garden, being 2.33 metres (7 feet 8 in) high including the coping tiles, and with an external facing of brick, one course thick, and an internal face of brick and flint cobble. These two sides are tied by cross bricks at regular intervals and would have presented a smart elevation facing the park and a more utilitarian one (possibly originally rendered) inside. The wall curves in and out along its length but not regularly enough to be termed a crinkle-crankle wall. Built into it, on the side facing the park, are two small buildings, clearly later additions.

Figure 107.
Internal wall of the menagerie behind the Bath House at Melton Constable. (Photo: Roger Last, 2015)

One is an earth-closet for the human inhabitants but the other, measuring 3.9 by 2.4 metres (12 foot 9 inches by 8 feet) and with three ventilated brick walls, one small window and a door to the menagerie's interior, may have been housing for animals or large birds. It is now used as a wood-store (Figure 108). The enclosure today

129

also contains the remains of an aviary, constructed of gault bricks, on the west side; and a former kennels building to the north-east, both nineteenth-century constructions. By 1826 Bryant's map (Figure 109) shows the menagerie grounds as almost rhomboid in shape, and containing several paths in a formal pattern. This map's accuracy, due to its small scale, is rather open to question, however, as Brown's kitchen garden and pleasure grounds to the east of the hall, the surrounding service buildings and the two fish ponds are not accurately depicted in terms of their shape or their spatial relationship with each other.

Figure 108.
External wall of the menagerie, overlooking the parkland. Built on to this wall is a later, ventilated building, with a door to the menagerie's interior, possibly for an animal or large birds? (Photograph: Roger Last, 2015)

Figure 109.
Detail of Bryant's 1826 map showing the hall and gardens in the centre and the menagerie near the trees on the left. (Private collection)

The Astley's menagerie is mentioned by several eighteenth- and nineteenth-century writers. The eighteenth century was a period in which private menageries flourished, as wealthy landowners vied with each other to collect exotic species from around the globe – an activity supported by a growing trade in imported animals, dead or alive. Not only did this intrigue their curiosity and the desire to learn about new species, but collecting the rare and unusual also boosted their social standing amongst their peers. A letter written (c.1730) by the 2nd Duke of Richmond, Charles Lennox to Sir Hans Sloane (Scientist, Physician and fellow Natural History collector) gives us an idea how landowners got caught up in the collecting frenzy and fell prey to unscrupulous animal traders.

> Sir
> I received your letter I am obliged to you for it. I wish indeed it
> had been the sloath [sic] that had been sent me,
> for that is the most curious animal I know;
> butt this is nothing butt a common young black bear,
> which I do not know what to do with,
> for I have five of them already. so pray when you write to him,
> I beg you would tell him not to send me any Bears, Eagles,
> Leopards, or Tygers, for I am overstock'd with them already.
> I am Dear Sir, Your Faithfull humble servant
> Richmond. [177]

Although local tales of alligators and other exotic creatures are still current in the locality, no written source describes any occupants of the menagerie at Melton Constable, other than beautiful or unusual birds!

Article 7 of the contract, which amongst other things bound Brown to 'level and adorn the ponds near the house with plantations etc', although listed last, would probably have been as costly and time-consuming as the digging out of the lake itself. It would have been a very large land-sculpting project, even if tackled with today's machinery. Sir Edward did not want to remove his fish ponds entirely but neither did he want them in close view of the hall. At first sight, it would appear that two of the four ponds or stews shown on the 1674 estate plan were filled in, but in reality the two middle ones were amalgamated and just the lower one was dispensed with. Perhaps cartloads of soil from the works at the lake were brought to the site, both to fill in the southern pond and to level the ground around the hall, stable yard and new kitchen and pleasure gardens' sites. The Victorian gardens built around the house have destroyed the graded landforms created by Brown, but the drawings made by Repton in 1781, Neale in 1818 (Figure 110) and Cotman, engraved by Webb in 1819 (Figure 111), all show smooth contouring bringing the parkland right up to the north, south and west elevations of the hall.

Figure 110.
Neale's 1818 engraving of Melton Constable Hall from the south-west. (Private collection)

Figure 111.
John Sell Cotman's 1819 engraving of Melton Constable Hall from the north-west. (Private collection)

Brown's phrase 'where the present kitchen garden stands' probably refers to the walled court shown due east of the 1680s house on Kip and Knyff's illustration. After the walls were dismantled this area became part of the new pleasure gardens bounded by the ha-ha. Once the land had been appropriately sculpted, Brown arranged more tree plantings, fringing the remaining ponds, and in the area in between the drive from the north-west and the parkland north-east of the stable yard.

After the last payment from Sir Edward Astley listed in Brown's account book, in December 1769, there appears to have been no more involvement by this eminent landscape architect. It is recorded that Sir Edward had to sell off part of the estate in 1768 to fund a very expensive election campaign and, although this was successful, this may explain why Brown was not called on to advise on any further 'improvements'.[178] However, the park continued to evolve during Sir Edward's lifetime. As mentioned above, road closure orders made in 1784 allowed the park to grow from 130 to 230 hectares (321 to 570 acres), particularly to the north, so that the house now stood more centrally in its landscape.[179] Belts of trees were established in this new northern addition beside the east–west road running along the park's northern boundary, leading towards Briston. As at Langley, however, much of the land lying within the expanded limits of the 'park' continued to be farmed as arable. Another renowned feature that Sir Edward developed, and one which is mentioned in most eighteenth- and nineteenth-century accounts of Melton Constable, is the folly known as 'Belle Vue' (sometimes anglicised to Belle View, Figure 112).

Figure 112.
1907 Postcard of Belle Vue folly or viewing tower (converted from a smock mill by Sir Edward Astley) in Briningham, a mile from the hall. (Private collection)

Originally built in 1721 by Sir Jacob Astley, 1st Baronet, as an octagonal, brick-based smock mill, it stands just inside the neighbouring parish of Briningham about 1.6 kilometres (1 mile) north of the hall. Probably the highest windmill (above sea level) erected in Norfolk, it also has the distinction of being the first to be converted into residential use. At some point between 1771 and 1780 Sir Edward replaced its wooden upper section with a three-storey, castellated brick tower topped by a conical cupola.[180] In 1781 Armstrong described how 'the tower, now called Belle-view . . . is commodiously fitted up; the apartments and furniture elegant and the look out at the top affords a prospect of sea and land twenty-five miles each way'.[181] Not only would this new observation point have provided the Astley family and their guests with panoramic prospects towards the North Norfolk coast but also far-reaching views inland, across their newly created Brownian landscape.

The *English Chronicle* in 1780–1 described Sir Edward Astley as 'open and affable in his manner, unaffected in his conversation, and generous and liberal in his principles . . . his judgements on occasions above mediocrity'. His parliamentary colleague Nathaniel Wraxhall described him as 'a man of no shining ability', yet one who 'justly excited respect as an upright country gentleman'. Astley said of himself: 'I do not propose myself to be of any party, or any side. I stand independent.'[182] Whatever his political leanings, he appears to have been well connected, and an important, familiar member of eighteenth-century Norfolk society. By employing Lancelot Brown to improve his park, he was firmly cementing his position in the midst of his political and county friends alike. After a 42-year tenure Sir Edward Astley died in March 1802 and the estate, and title, passed to his eldest son, Sir Jacob Astley.

Melton Constable since 1802

Sir Jacob, 5th Baronet (1756–1817), undertook a considerable building programme during his relatively short time as the owner of Melton Constable. He built the hall's eastern corridor to connect the detached service wing – the former Tudor remnant – which became the core of today's north wing. The Georgian sash windows, second-floor dormers, square chimney stacks and brick pilasters adorning the western elevation of the building hide the older structure within. The stable yard behind, as already discussed, still contains at least three of the buildings shown on the 1674 estate map. Sir Jacob adapted these and added to their number, thus developing an elaborate enclosed stable yard. All the buildings have arched detailing in the brick or rendered walls, and those ranged on either side of the clock-tower entrance also feature recessed ground-floor front walls behind a pillared colonnade. The appearance of the early nineteenth-century stable buildings and the clock tower over the gateway have been compared to the work of Sir John Soane, who was active in Norfolk at the time but who cannot, as yet, be directly linked to Melton Constable. The two lodge gates – Swanton Gate Lodge on the B1110 and the Church Lodge by St Peter's Church – were also built around this date in a classical style. It is thought that Sir Jacob added to the pleasure ground by planting a diverse range of tree species to form an arboretum.[183]

By the time the pleasure grounds were depicted, liberally planted, on the Tithe Award Map of 1850, the trees planted here by Brown would have been well established. In this same year James Grigor published *The Eastern Arboretum*, in it he observes:

> The park here consists of many hundreds of acres and is surrounded by a belt, which has been judiciously added to in some places and lessened in others, so as in a great degree to take off that hoop-like uniformity which belts are so prone to create. The pine tribe is throughout far too predominant and exhibit a very ragged and meagre appearance.

He remarks that for a park of such a great age there is not one single tree of 'extraordinary dimensions', which is surprising, particularly in those areas that had been deer park since at least 1674. He also complains about a stone wall running on the inside of the wooded belts spoiling the 'flowing and undefined outline of the sylvan scenery'. Grigor does, however, mention some fine specimens of cedar of Lebanon and Portuguese laurel in the Dress Ground and Menagerie, and silver firs in the woods.[184]

Sometime after the Tithe Map was surveyed, but before the publication of the Ordnance Survey First Edition 6-inch map in 1885 (Figure 113 shows the OS 1900s edition), the ground immediately around the main house was formed into a series of terraces for an Italianate formal garden. Stone steps lead down from the south door to three circular, formal beds, each containing a fountain. The new ornamental garden was surrounded by stone balustrading, surmounted by numerous stone urns and planters (Figure 114). Matching balustrading appears to have been erected around the Bath House, to judge from a photograph of 1905.[185] As described above, the southern end of Brown's ha-ha was filled in at this time, allowing the pleasure garden and arboretum to expand southwards at the expense of the park. Two square areas of sunken lawn were created here, presumably for playing croquet or bowls or entertaining outside. The Italianate garden was featured as an illustration in Morris's *Country Seats* of 1880 (Figure 115). This image shows that the octagonal banqueting house associated with the Tudor house still survived at this time; it also depicts the enormous portico, added to the north elevation around 1817, to provide shelter for arriving carriages and their occupants.

135

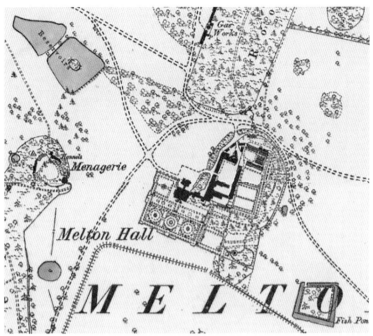

Figure 113.
Detail of the hall, menagerie, Italianate garden terracing, service buildings and the extensive number of glasshouses in the kitchen garden. (Reproduced from the Ordnance Survey 1885 First Edition 6-inch to the mile map with kind permission of the Ordnance Survey)

Figure 114.
1896 photograph taken from the south-east corner of the Italianate Garden by the Hon. Derek W.G. Keppel, Royal Equerry and Master of the Royal Household. (Norfolk Records Office: MC 2615/2)

Figure 115.
Illustration by Alexander Lydon from William Orpen Morris 'County Seats of the Noblemen and Gentlemen of Great Britain and Ireland', 1870.

Neither of these two structures have survived to the present day, which in the case of the banqueting house at least, is a great pity. The late nineteenth-century Ordnance Survey map also show at least three landing piers on the lake, a boathouse on the southern end of the north shore, and a teahouse – surrounded by Teahouse Plantation – on the west shore (Figure 116).

Figure 116.
1905 postcard showing the teahouse at Melton Constable's lake. (Private collection)

137

This same map depicts the considerable number of glasshouses and cold frames that then occupied the kitchen garden. Many of these survive to this day but are in need of a fair amount of restoration before their glass can be reinstated. The rusting remains of a boiler behind the north wall's glasshouses, and the empty boiler pit next to a bothy with its lean-to glasshouse, are reminders of the exotic fruit and flowers grown for the house in its heyday.

In 1881 Sir George Manners Astley, 20th Baron Hastings (1857–1904) made 25 acres of land available in the north of the estate (along with part of Burgh Parva) for the location of the Midland and Great Northern railway works and station buildings, stipulating that this was on condition that a private waiting room was built, for use by himself and the nobility, at the Lynn end of the station.[186] As the photograph below shows, Sir George held weekend and shooting parties on his estate, entertaining a wide circle of influential and high society guests.

Figure 117.
October 1896 photograph of Sir George Manners – standing fifth from the left – and his guests in front of a rustic summer house (possibly the circular building in the arboretum, shown on the 1885 OS map?). The party most notably included TRH Duke and Duchess of York (future King George V and Queen Mary) standing on either side of Sir George. (From a photo album belonging to Hon. Derek W.G. Keppel. Norfolk Records Office: MC 2615/2)

Towards the end of the nineteenth century the park was enlarged slightly to the south-west, to allow for the construction of the Jubilee Gates (or Dereham Gates) and the laying out of a new section of drive leading through Wood Severals to the South Lodge. Melton Constable Park continued to flourish until, like many large estates, it was assailed by a cocktail of economic and social challenges in the early decades of the twentieth century. Sir Albert Edward Delaval Astley, 21st Baron Hastings (1882–1956) wanted to concentrate his finance on renovating his other residence at Seaton Delaval in Northumberland, and so sold Melton Constable to the Duke of Westminster in 1948. The Duke in turn sold the hall and park in 1959 to Geoffrey Harrold who wished to farm much of the land, and the house remained uninhabited for a long period. In 1986, the hall, terraced garden, stable yard, kitchen garden, Bath House and associated cottages were sold to Roger Gawn, thus severing the centuries old link between the house and park. In recent years a new pond has been dug on the site of the medieval fish pond filled in by Lancelot Brown and several of the buildings on the site have been turned into residential units. The future of the Grade I listed hall is uncertain, several of the other buildings mentioned in the text are either Grade II or II* listed and at varying stages of renovation. The Deer Park is a Grade II* registered landscape. However, despite the intervening 250 years or more, it is certain that Lancelot Brown would recognise his landscape 'improvements' at Melton Constable, the majority of which are still very much in evidence today.

Figure 118.
View of the hall from across the lake – Melton Constable Park is still a Brownian landscape today. (Photo: Roger Last, 2013)

CHAPTER 5 OTHER NORFOLK PARKS ASSOCIATED WITH BROWN

Langley, Kimberley, and Melton Constable are the only landscapes in Norfolk that we can say with absolute confidence were designed by Capability Brown. There is, however, one other place in the county where Brown appears to have worked, although apparently only on a small scale; two others where his involvement in the landscape has been suggested; and one further case where there are faint, tantalising suggestions of a possible connection. Something must be said briefly about these puzzling places, and also about the vexed question of who it was, precisely, who designed all the other landscape parks in eighteenth-century Norfolk.

Holkham Park (©Mike Page Aerial Photography)

Holkham

Holkham is the only place in Norfolk, other than the three main sites discussed in this volume, where Brown almost certainly advised on improvements. The client was Margaret Coke (Figure 119), the widow of Thomas Coke, first Earl of Leicester, who had – earlier in the century – been responsible for building the

Figure 119.
Portrait of Lady Margaret Tufton, First Countess of Leicester, by Andrea Casali (By kind permission of the 8th Earl of Leicester and the trustees of the Holkham Estate)

magnificent Palladian mansion of Holkham Hall. Brown's involvement here is hardly surprising. Holkham was one of the largest estates in the county and the landscape laid out around the hall was, during the course of the eighteenth and nineteenth centuries, worked on by a string of famous landscape designers including William Kent, Humphry Repton and William Andrews Nesfield.[187] Moreover, the park as it is today – the largest in Norfolk – has, in many ways, a very 'Brownian' appearance, with a slightly serpentine lake to the north-west of the hall, a continuous perimeter belt, numerous clumps and – in Obelisk Wood to the south of the hall – an elegant classical temple and obelisk. The hall itself was built between 1734 and 1760 and was designed, like many large houses in the first half of the eighteenth century, by a group of men: Thomas Coke himself, the Norwich architect Matthew Brettingham, the famous amateur architect Lord Burlington, and William Kent. Through the 1720s and 1730s an elaborate landscape, which

142

combined (in the manner of the times) both geometric and 'naturalistic' elements, was gradually laid out around the hall, in part to designs by Kent. It included Obelisk Wood, crowning the low hill some 500 metres (546 yards) to the south of the hall, which was dissected by a network of ruler-straight allées focused on the temple and obelisk already noted; the great lake, which went through a number of changes; and the south approach, extending in a direct line for some 3 kilometres (1.8 miles) as far as an entrance lodge designed by Kent.[188] Formal lines of trees extended south from the hall as far as Obelisk Wood, but the area close to the south front was laid out by Kent, from the late 1730s, in an irregular, 'naturalistic' manner, with an artificial hillock, the 'New Mount', surmounted by a temple-like seat, and a 'serpentine river' which led to the lake.[189] Although the landscape was thus complex and sophisticated, the park itself at Holkham was not large at this time. When Thomas Coke died in 1759 it covered no more than 150 hectares, and did not extend to the south of Obelisk Wood. What is now the southern half of the park, and much of its eastern and western sections, did not yet exist; the continuous outer belt had not yet been planted; and the great ovoid clumps which today grace much of the parkland had not been established (Figure 120).

It is sometimes suggested that all these features were the work of Brown himself. Indeed, some texts even attribute the lake, or at least its current serpentine shape, to him. But the payments made by Margaret Coke (née Tufton), the First Countess of Leicester in 1762 were apparently small and Humphry Repton – who laid out a pleasure ground by the lake at Holkham in 1789, and probably knew what he was talking about – suggests that Brown's direct activity here was limited. In his book, *Sketches and Hints on Landscape Gardening* (1796), he describes how Brown was succeeded by:

> A numerous herd of his foremen and working gardeners, who, from having executed his designs, became consulted, as well as employed, in the several works which he had entrusted them to superintend. Among these, one person had deservedly acquired great credit at Harewood, at Holkham, and other places, by the execution of gravel walks, the planting of shrubberies, and other details belonging to pleasure grounds, which were generally divided from the park by a sunk fence, or ha! ha! and happy would it have been for the country, and the art, if he had confined his talents within such boundary. Unfortunately, without the same great ideas, he fancied he might improve by enlarging his plans.

> This introduced all that bad taste which has been attributed to his
> great master, Brown.[190]

This suggests that Brown's 'improvements' at Holkham were limited in scale. They may have included the removal of internal divisions within the park, and perhaps of some of the more formal features surviving from the work of William Kent. But they were largely focused on the area near the hall; did not embrace the entire landscape; and were largely executed, and perhaps even in part designed, by one of his 'foremen'. The individual concerned was probably Adam Mickle, who worked with Brown – on and off – from 1757 until 1779, and who was certainly involved – together with his son, Adam junior – in the landscape at Harewood. However precisely responsibility for the design of the pleasure ground was divided, it is clear that Brown can have had little part in creating the Holkham landscape as we see it today, for the simple reason that the expansion of the park to its present limits, the planting of the belt and clumps, and the transformation of the lake along more fashionable, serpentine lines did not take place under Margaret Coke at all, or even under her successor, Coke's nephew Wenman Coke, but rather under Thomas William Coke, who only inherited the estate in 1776.

Figure 120.
Aerial photo taken from the south of the Holkham Estate showing the Brownian clumps of trees. (©Mike Page Aerial Photography)

Work on improving and extending the park appears to have begun in 1780, when a number of roads in the locality were closed or diverted, followed by further closures and diversions in 1782.[191] In the same year William Emes was commissioned to give the northern end of the lake a fashionable serpentine 'twist'.[192] Emes was one of Brown's most successful competitors, and designed numerous parks and pleasure grounds, mainly in the Midlands.[193] So far as the evidence goes Emes' work at Holkham was limited to altering the lake. The expansion of the park, and the planting of the clumps and belts, was the responsibility of one John Sandys, who is first recorded working at Holkham in the previous year (1781). He nevertheless appears to have had some connection with Emes, for he was probably the son of the head gardener at Kedleston in Derbyshire, where Emes himself had worked on the grounds in the late 1750s, in part under the direction of the architect Robert Adam.[194] In 1801 his brother Charles Sandys advertised his services as a garden designer and boasted that he had worked as 'foreman to Mr Eames'.[195] John Sandys was appointed to the post of head gardener at Holkham, and planted more than two million trees in a sustained campaign which lasted from 1781 until 1805, carefully recording in a notebook the numbers and species of trees in every clump, and in every section of the new perimeter belt. Not every change made to the landscape in this period can be attributed to him. The creation of a further serpentine 'twist' to the lake, this time at its southern end, in 1802 was the work of John Webb, a former pupil of William Emes, while Humphry Repton was employed here in 1789, at an early stage of his career, to lay out a pleasure ground beside the lake.[196] But Sandys appears to have presided over the key changes.

Although the area described by contemporaries as 'Holkham park' was thus considerably expanded – so that it became the largest park in Norfolk, covering an area of more than 10 square kilometres (c.3.8 square miles) – as at Langley and Melton Constable much of the land within the perimeter belt continued, in fact, to be farmed as arable, and even divided into fields, as seen on Figure 120. Indeed, the estate's home farm – Longlands – itself lay within the belt, just to the north-west of the new southern entrance. This immense landscaping project was, so far as we know, the only one undertaken by Sandys, who continued to work at Holkham until 1805, when he retired and the following year married the forty-six-year-old widow of a Dutch sea captain in the nearby town of Wells-next-the-Sea.[197] The couple continued to live there, accumulating and managing a portfolio of properties, with Sandys himself providing advice on forestry for, amongst other places, the Blickling estate.[198] It might be thought that, rather than being responsible for this grand design, Sandys was in reality merely carrying out a long-term plan, conceived on an ambitious scale by William Emes himself. However, disputing this theory are the words proudly written on the cover of Sandys' own notebook: 'the plantations designed and planted by John Sandys'.[199]

In spite of numerous subsequent changes and additions to the landscape, most notably the immense terraced gardens, designed by William Andrews Nesfield, which were constructed around the hall in the 1850s, the Holkham landscape retains, for the most part, an eighteenth-century, 'Brownian' appearance. But this is not due to Brown himself, but rather to the work of his predecessor William Kent, to Emes and Webb, and above all to Sandys. Whatever the extent and character of Brown's involvement in the pleasure grounds, no trace of his activities survives today, due to the drastic remodelling of the area in the middle of the nineteenth century.

Figure 121.
Aerial photograph of Wolterton Park taken from the north. (©Mike Page Aerial Photography)

Wolterton and Ditchingham: dubious attributions

A number of writers have suggested that Brown was involved in remodelling the landscape at Wolterton in north Norfolk.[200] This is superficially plausible, given that Wolterton Hall was a residence of some importance and one at which two other noted landscape designers are known to have worked: Charles Bridgeman, who originally laid out the grounds in the 1720s; and William Sawrey Gilpin, who gave them a picturesque 'makeover' in the late 1820s. But the Brown attribution rests entirely on a single source, Gilpin himself, who refers to Brown's activities at Wolterton twice in his book of 1832, *Practical Hints upon Landscape Gardening*. Both references concern the prospect from the south front of the house. In the first passage Gilpin criticises the way in which Brown sometimes enclosed a large area of ground with a ha-ha, which extended beyond – and was itself separated by another ha-ha – the 'dress lawn' of the pleasure ground. This separate area of parkland, was, by implication, mown for hay rather than grazed, and it was framed on either side by plantations, through which a circuit path 'leads you round the confines of this cheerless patch of coarse grass'.[201] Such an arrangement could, he suggests, be seen both at Wolterton in Norfolk, and at Kirtlington in Oxfordshire. A little later in the book he returned to this theme:

> This necessity of life and motion to constitute cheerfulness is manifested in several places laid out by Brown, where a lawn, surrounded by a sunk fence, and closed on two sides with corresponding rows of trees like blinkers, being left in a state of nature, but unoccupied by cattle, throws a veil of monotonous dullness over the scene, which no ray of cheerfulness can penetrate. Such was the case at Wolterton in Norfolk, and at Kirtlington Park, near Woodstock.[202]

At both places the deficiency had, Gilpin explained, now been remedied by his own work, at Wolterton by constructing the great transverse terrace that still survives below the south front of the house, and by planting clumps of shrubs within the area of the lawn.

Kirtlington was unquestionably one of Brown's designs – he worked there between 1751 and 1757, one of his earliest commissions. But there is no other evidence that Brown was involved at Wolterton. The arrangement of lawn, flanked by planting, which Gilpin criticised had in fact been established much earlier, by Charles Bridgeman in the 1720s (Figure 122). It was part of an extensive but simple geometric landscape, featuring a large lake to the south of the house, typical of Bridgeman's work, and of its period, which was laid out around Wolterton Hall, built for Horatio Walpole, Lord Orford, the brother of Sir Robert Walpole of Houghton.[203] Through the 1730s and 1740s the Wolterton landscape was progressively simplified by Horatio, in line with contemporary fashions, and the

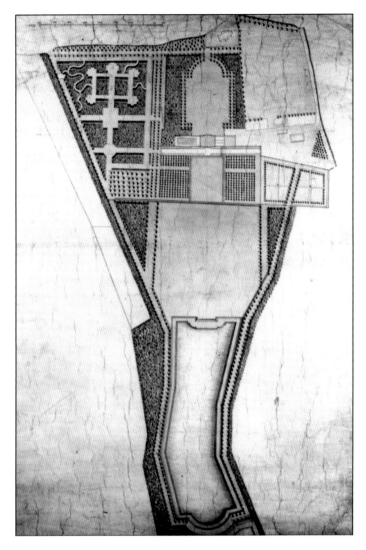

Figure 122.
Charles Bridgeman's design for the gardens at Wolterton Hall, 1728. (Bodleian Library, Oxford)

park much extended, especially to the east. Nevertheless, an undated map from the mid-1740s shows the house still set in grounds characterised by serried ranks of trees, framing rigid vistas to north and south.[204] Horatio died in 1757, and was succeeded by his son, also Horatio, who became First Lord Orford (of the second creation) and lived until 1809. It was he who would have called in Brown to modernise the grounds, and a map surveyed in the year of his death certainly shows that changes had been made.[205] Some new areas of woodland had been established,

148

and the rigidity of the landscape much softened. The somewhat sparse estate archives which survive from this period describe new planting in the 1760s and 1770s, much of it in the park rather than the pleasure grounds. It featured indigenous broad-leafed species like oak and ash but also significant quantities of Scots pine, silver fir and spruce. Willows and 'Turin' (i.e. Lombardy) poplar were also planted – a hundred of the latter in 1778 alone.[206] The Wolterton landscape was thus brought up to date in the second half of the eighteenth century but, while it is by no means impossible that Brown advised on improvements, Gilpin's comments are our only indication of this. No payments from Walpole to Brown are recorded in the latter's bank accounts, no mention of Brown appears in surviving documents at the hall, and no other commentator in the eighteenth or nineteenth centuries appear to have associated Brown and Wolterton. This is a fine landscape, with magnificent views south across Bridgeman's beautiful lake, much embellished by Gilpin's planting[207] (Figure 123). But on balance, it probably owes nothing to Brown.

Figure 123.
One of William Sawrey Gilpin's designs for improving the lake at Wolterton in 'picturesque' fashion, c.1830. (Private Collection)

Figure 124.
Aerial photo of Ditchingham Park taken from the north-east. (©Mike Page Aerial Photography)

A third park in Norfolk sometimes claimed as the work of Brown – Ditchingham, in the far south-east of the county – is even less likely to have been designed by him. It is attributed to the great man by no less an authority than Nicholas Pevsner in his volume on the architecture of Norfolk, and it is included in a number of published lists of Brown's works.[208]   But other authorities have been more cautious. Jane Brown for example, in her excellent biography of Brown, suggests that the attribution is no more than a 'family tradition'.[209]   It is true that the beautifully preserved park, one of the most visually appealing in the county, has a very 'Brownian' appearance, with its fine serpentine lake created by damming a minor tributary of the river Waveney, known as the Broome Beck, and with wooded ground rising behind it. The park was considered fashionable enough to be engraved by John Butcher in 1778 [210] (Figure 125). His view shows the house – standing on a low hill to the west of the lake – in the distance; some kind of Gothick building hidden in trees to the right; a bridge of fashionable open-work design spanning the lower end of the lake; and a garden building apparently standing on an island at its upper end. The scene appears even more 'Brownian' in character than the modern landscape at Ditchingham.

150

Figure 125.
Engraving of Ditchingham Hall and Park by John Butcher, 1778. (Private collection)

Ditchingham Hall was built around 1710 for the Revd John James Bedingfeld, replacing an earlier house, shown on a map of 1615, which occupied roughly the same site.[211] The estate remained in the family's possession until the late nineteenth century. A map of 1713 shows the hall set in an elaborate geometric landscape, which, by the time a second map was surveyed in 1764, had undergone a number of modifications.[212] Both maps, however, show that the main area of ornamental walled gardens lay to the east of the house, on the sloping ground leading down to the Broome Beck, where there was a building, possibly a bathhouse, beside the stream. The 1764 map appears to have been made prior to the 'deformalisation' of the grounds, for it includes a marginal text which details the relative heights of various features depicted, as well as marking out the more 'prominent trees', which were presumably to be retained when the grounds were converted into something more fashionably 'naturalistic'. Another feature retained may have been the building shown beside the stream, for the structure standing below the house on Butcher's engraving appears to occupy the same site, although now apparently converted into an island in the lake.

There are persistent rumours that a design for the park, signed by Brown, still exists. But nobody appears to have seen it for many years. The Bedingfelds were not the kind of major landowner, or wealthy London businessman, for whom Brown usually worked, but a Norfolk gentry family who possessed a relatively modest estate, and there are no references to them in Brown's account book (which deals with commissions started in the early 1760s) and no receipts from the family

151

are recorded in his bank accounts. The 1764 map is signed by one Joseph Rumball, who is not known as an associate of Brown. He was a surveyor who prepared maps and plans of a number of estates in Norfolk and at least one in Wiltshire between 1748 and 1773, and who appears to have served for a while as bailiff to the governors of the Great Hospital, Norwich.[213] On balance, then, there seems little to associate Brown with Ditchingham, although it was clearly a landscape at the cutting edge of fashion in the 1760s, and thus contemporary with Brown's work at Melton Constable and Langley. As a consequence of its gently rolling topography and the presence close by of an eminently dammable watercourse, it represents a more complete expression of Brown's ideas than either of these places (Figure 126).

Figure 126.
Ditchingham Park, one of the finest eighteenth-century parks in Norfolk, is often attributed to Brown, but was almost certainly designed by someone else. (Photo: Tom Williamson)

West Tofts and Buckenham Tofts: a puzzle

A further site, or perhaps more accurately sites, must be briefly mentioned: Buckenham Tofts and West Tofts, side by side in the arid Breckland district of south-west Norfolk. Both mansions are now demolished and their sites are incorporated within the Battle Training Area, where what remains of their parks are looked after with surprising care by the military.[214] A new hall (Figure 127) was built at Buckenham Tofts by one 'Mr. Vincent', a London excise official, in the late seventeenth century, and a fine map of c.1700 shows that this was surrounded by elaborate formal gardens (with a canal and garden building, perhaps adapted from the redundant church) and had a diminutive deer park, covering some 15 hectares, immediately to the east[215] (Figure 128).

Figure 127.
Edwardian postcard of Buckenham Tofts Hall, as remodelled by Samuel Wyatt at the start of the nineteenth century. (Private collection)

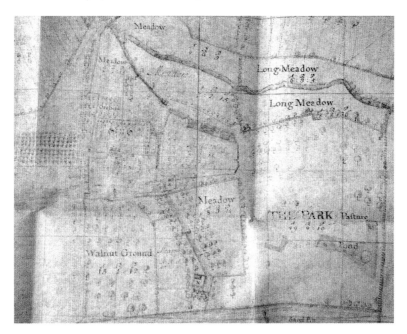

Figure 128.
Detail from the c.1700 estate map of Buckenham Tofts. (Norfolk Records Office, PTR 3/3 758 X1. Photo: Roger Last 2016)

Following Vincent's death in c.1700 the estate passed through a number of hands before being acquired by Phillip Howard, the brother of the Duke of Norfolk, in 1736. A survey drawn up around 1760 suggests that the house remained largely unchanged, and that the, by now, unfashionable walled gardens still survived intact.[216] Around the same time (probably in 1763) the property passed to the Petre family, whose main residence was at Westwick in the east of the county, following the marriage of Phillip Howard's daughter to the 9th Baron Petre. It was under the Petres that the park appears to have been expanded into a landscape park, with a lake, wooded belts and clumps of trees, extending over an area of some 2.5 square kilometres or nearly a square mile.

Breckland, where land was cheap and the shooting good, was densely studded with gentleman's seats in the eighteenth century and next door to Buckenham Tofts lay the estate of West Tofts, where sometime around 1770 a new mansion was erected by Mr George Nelson. Shortly afterwards he sold the estate to Stephen Payne-Gallwey, who probably expanded a park established by Nelson. The two men – Payne-Gallwey and Lord Petre – appear to have developed the landscape to some extent together, closing and diverting roads and undertaking an extensive programme of tree planting, mainly in order to improve the shooting, although in the face of unrelenting depredations by the Breckland rabbits.[217] None of this would be relevant to our theme if it wasn't for a single letter surviving in the archives at Norfolk Record Office, dated 10 April 1788, in which Payne-Gallwey reported to Lord Petre how he had been the previous day to 'Tofts':

> Purposely to see what had been done in consequence of the Orders I had given to follow Mr Lapidge's Plan, but did not return in time for the post. I am almost ashamed to say it was the first Time I had been there for a Month I confess the Interval between the ground to be planted on my side appears (now done) much longer than I had any idea of. And if it is an Object with your Lordship I shall be ready to do anything you wish. But when I first proposed the matter to your Lordship I confess I thought I had consulted the little Beauty the Place is capable of receiving as well as the Advantage of Sporting. When Lapidge suggested a different Plan to me I approv[e]d his Plan in Prefer[e]nce to my own & thinking it a Matter of total Indifference to your Lordship (from its being the Extremity of the Estate & remote from the House at Buckenham) I ventur[e]d to direct Lapidge's Plan to be follow[e]d

& desir[e]d Rix might be inform[e]d immediately of what I directed to be done.[218]

'Lapidge' is none other than Samuel Lapidge (1740–1806), who joined Brown's team in 1767 and continued to work with him until his death in 1783, when he was named in his will as his successor in the business.[219] Lapidge, 'who knows my accounts' (quote from Brown's will), was to complete any contracts currently in progress; and this he duly did at Chalfont and Bulstrode in Buckinghamshire and Sandleford Priory in Berkshire. It is just possible that his work at 'Tofts' represents another of Brown's unfinished commissions.

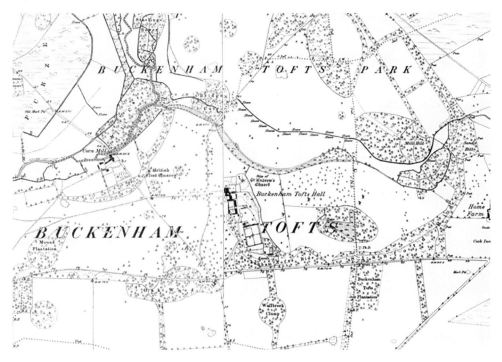

Figure 129.
1883 OS 6-inch map of Buckenham Tofts Park. (Ordnance Survey 6-inch series 1883, by kind permission of the Ordnance Survey)

The wording of the letter implies that the planting, which was apparently on the boundary between the two properties, was made to Lapidge's own design, and he certainly undertook some work on his own account, even while Brown was still alive. This said, it is unlikely that he would have been brought in by the two landowners merely to establish a plantation, and the project described may have followed on from earlier work at either West Tofts or Buckenham Tofts. The

Ordnance Survey draft 2-inch drawings from the nineteenth century make it clear that Buckenham Tofts was a very 'Brownian' landscape featuring not only clumps, serpentine lake and belts but also numerous rides and drives.[220] West Tofts was less obviously 'Brownian' in appearance but it was largely enclosed by a great perimeter belt, which soon became a notable feature of the bleak local landscape. This was already in place by 1780, when Nelson sold the estate, for it is described in the sales catalogue of that date.[221] It was later said to have been planted in the 1770s by Mr Griffin, a nurseryman of nearby Mundford, and elsewhere in the letter from Payne-Gallwey to Petre, quoted above, Griffin's name is mentioned in association with the ongoing improvements in 1787.[222] The belt had a 'most agreeable ride' laid out down its centre.[223] Lapidge's presence in the middle of Breckland in the 1780s remains something of a mystery but may just suggest the earlier involvement of Brown with one or other of the Tofts – probably Buckenham – as in 1789 Humphry Repton was to give some advice on the grounds there.

Brown and the Norfolk Landscape

Even if further research were to reveal that Brown was involved at either of these Breckland sites, *and* that Gilpin's suggestions about Wolterton were correct, this would still bring the total number of places in Norfolk where Lancelot Brown worked to only five. We do not know how many parks existed in the county when Brown died in 1783 but a little over a decade later, when William Faden surveyed his map of the county, there were no less than 119 examples covering an area greater than 15 hectares (37 acres), ranging from vast designs like Holkham to numerous diminutive 'lawns' laid out around small manor houses and 'villas' (Figure 130). It is true that some of these will have come into existence since the time of Brown's death; it is also the case that over half were owned by the kinds of people who could not possibly have afforded to employ the great man. But even allowing for this, it is evident that Brown was responsible for only a small proportion of the landscape parks which had been created in Norfolk by the time of his death.

The county has, in fact, fewer of Brown's works for its size than many others in England: most of his commissions were in the Home Counties and in the south and west Midlands. The distribution of Brown's work broadly mirrors that of wealthy residences in England in the second half of the eighteenth century, which were concentrated around London and, to a lesser but increasing extent, in the industrial areas of the Midlands and the north-west.

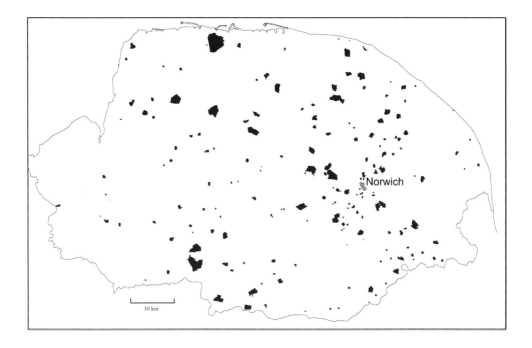

Figure 130.
The distribution of landscape parks shown on Williams Faden's map of Norfolk, published in 1797. (courtesy of Andrew Macnair)

CHAPTER 6   EIGHTEENTH-CENTURY PARKS IN NORFOLK: THE WIDER LEGACY

Brown's rivals

If Brown and his team were responsible for only a fraction of Norfolk's eighteenth-century parks, who designed the rest? As we noted in the first chapter, a number of contemporary landscape gardeners, although never as successful or as sought-after as Brown, nevertheless acquired national reputations, and operated on a national scale. Many originally worked with Brown before setting up as designers in their own right, like the unnamed individual castigated by Repton who had worked with Brown at Holkham: 'foremen and working gardeners' with ideas above their station, 'the day labourers who became his successors' and 'illiterate followers' who diluted and corrupted Brown's style.[224] But the designs of such men could be as impressive as anything created by Brown. One of the most successful was Nathaniel Richmond, who probably met Brown when he was improving the grounds of Warwick Castle in the early 1750s and was certainly working with him by 1754, laying out the new pleasure ground for Lord Anson at Moor Park in Hertfordshire.[225] He was part of Brown's team at a number of places, including Syon Park in Middlesex, but in 1759 he set up on his own as a landscape designer and nurseryman in Marylebone.[226] Soon afterwards we find him designing a new park at Marden Park in Surrey; in 1762 he was at Stoke Park, Stoke Poges, in Buckinghamshire; and in 1763 he began work at Danson Park near Bexley in Kent and at Shardeloes near Amersham in Buckinghamshire. By the time of his death (of septicaemia) in February 1784 he had worked at more than thirty places in England, including Himley in Staffordshire, Saltram near Plymouth, Stanmer House in Sussex, Escot House and Eggesford in Devon, Eastbourne Place in Sussex, Hitchin Priory in Hertfordshire and Badminton in Gloucestershire. Humphry Repton, setting out on his own career as landscape gardener in 1788, described how 'the works of Kent, Brown and Richmond have been the places of my worship'.[227]

Richmond worked at Beeston St Lawrence near Wroxham relatively late in his career, in the mid-1770s. A small park – a diminutive deer enclosure – had existed here as early as 1756 but Jacob Preston, who remodelled the hall in 'Gothick' style between 1773 and 1777, evidently wanted to provide his new home with a more fashionable setting[228] (Figure 131). The estate accounts record thirteen payments for visits by Richmond between January 1774 and January 1778, and Preston's

Figure. 131
Neale's engraving of Beeston St Lawrence. (Private Collection)

brother-in-law, Henry Hulton, described in 1776 in a letter to his sister how the grounds were being modernised 'by one of the gentleman improvers', who was demolishing the old walled gardens and laying out a new kitchen garden 'more remote from the house'.[229]   A narrow, serpentine lake, ranged roughly north-west/south-east, was created to the south of the mansion by damming a tributary of the river Ant, and the park was extended so that it covered around 95 hectares (c.230 acres). It was surrounded by belts of trees along its western, northern and eastern sides and was internally subdivided by a ha-ha (Figure 132). A serpentine carriage drive led to the house – standing roughly in the centre of the park – from the Norwich road to the west, crossing the lake by a bridge. The lake, and some of the perimeter belts, still survive, although most of the planting within the park was destroyed when the land was ploughed in the second half of the twentieth century (it has since been returned to grass). The walls of Richmond's kitchen garden also remain, some 250 metres to the north of the hall, still screened by belts of trees, together with a fine orangery which stands between the two, within the pleasure grounds, which was apparently part of the same programme of 'improvements'. So far there is no evidence that Richmond worked anywhere else in Norfolk – only one other commission is known in East Anglia, at Woolverstone in Suffolk – but more of his work may yet come to light.

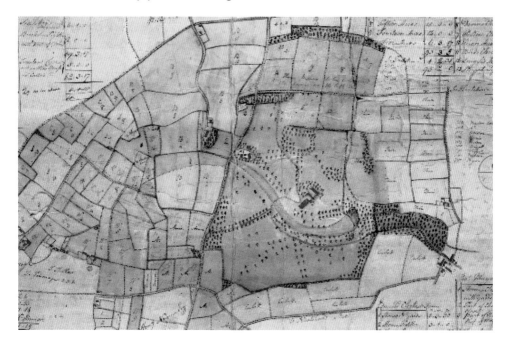

Figure 132.
An undated estate map, c.1785, showing the park and lake at Beeston St Lawrence in north-east Norfolk, designed in the previous decade by Nathaniel Richmond. (Private collection)

Other landscape designers, rivals to Brown and operating on a national scale, differed from Richmond in that they never appear to have been part of Brown's circle. The most famous and successful was Richard Woods, an Essex-based designer and nurseryman who was responsible for at least 40 commissions, mainly in the south-east of the country, and who was actually employed in preference to Brown by Lord Arundel at Wardour Castle in Wiltshire in 1771.[230] Woods, however, does not appear to have received any Norfolk commissions. Less successful was Samuel Driver, a Kentish nurseryman who provided designs for places as far apart as Belhus in Essex (in 1764) and Adlestrop in Gloucestershire (c.1762).[231] In 1773 he was commissioned by Sir Martin Browne Ffolkes, who had recently inherited the Hillington estate in north-west Norfolk, to remodel the grounds of the hall. Driver's plan, which survives in the Norfolk Record Office, features a narrow lake lying to the south of the house, clumps of trees on mounds and a serpentine drive, and serpentine walks, running through a near-continuous perimeter belt[232] (Figure 133). The design appears rather old-fashioned for its date, certainly when compared with the one he had produced for Belhus nine years earlier, and the plan itself seems somewhat stylised in character.

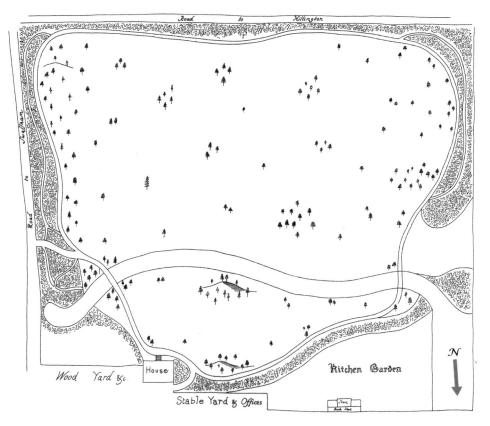

Figure 133.
Driver's 1773 plan for Hillington Park. (Sketch taken from the original in the Norfolk Record Office, ref: NRS 21369. Tom Williamson)

A landscape park was created around Hillington at this time, and the estate accounts record in some detail the money spent on demolishing the old walled gardens, stubbing out hedges and grassing down a wide area of former arable land around the house. Many trees were planted, including 300 Scots pines in 1776 and a thousand sweet chestnuts in 1777.[233] The work continued for more than two decades, costing Ffolkes an average of more than £100 per annum. As shown on the earliest available map – the tithe award of 1838 – and the 1884 Ordnance Survey 6-inch map, the park does not much resemble Driver's design, not least in

162

that the lake as created lay to the north of the mansion, rather than to the south[234] (Figure 134). However, there are some similarities in the overall distribution of the belts; Driver was paid, in 1774, for laying out a shrubbery and supplying the plants;[235] and it is possible that – although much of his initial plan was rejected – Driver may have designed and supervised the creation of this new landscape.

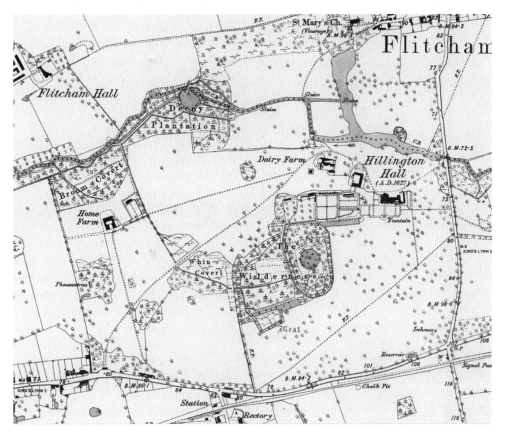

Figure 134.
OS 6-inch map of Hillington Park. (Reproduced from Ordnance Survey one-inch 1884 map with the kind permission of the Ordnance Survey)

Local Practitioners

Other designers of national importance who worked in the county in the eighteenth century are few in number, before the start of Humphry Repton's career in 1788. Williams Emes, who we have already met at Holkham, more or less completes the list. Who, then, was responsible for the majority of the landscape parks created in the county in this period? The simple answer is that in most cases we do not know.

163

It is clear that a number of individuals advertised their services as garden designers in Norfolk in the middle and later decades of the century. One, slightly before Brown's rise to fame, was George Wynn, who described himself as both 'Gardener' and 'Land Surveyor' in an advertisement placed in the *Norwich Mercury* in 1747, in which he offered to:

> Form, plan, and set out Gentlemen's Gardens, in a modern and complete Manner, according to the true Method of designing . . . He will likewise agree with Gentlemen to keep their Gardens by the Year, and supply them with Fruit, Forrest-Trees, Flowering Shrubs etc.[236]

A little later, in 1752, Henry Ellison, likewise based in Norwich and describing himself as both gardener and land surveyor, informed the readers of the *Mercury* that 'notwithstanding many Reports unfairly spread to the contrary' he undertook:

> All Sorts of Gardening Works, Wood-Works, Forest Planting, and Planting in all branches whatsoever, in altering old Gardens, as well as making new ones . . . all which he completely finishes after the most modern Taste, and reasonable prices.[237]

The list of features he offered to provide still included geometric ones like avenues, wildernesses and parterres, as well as more modern elements like 'Serpentine Rivers', but if his business continued far into the 1750s his designs, if they were to remain fashionable, presumably developed along more naturalistic lines. More clearly in the 'Brownian' mode – or so we can assume given his earlier career – were the offerings of Samuel Gooch, who announced in February 1764 in the *Norwich Mercury* that he was 'now arrived from London' and settled in Norwich with an intention to undertake 'New Work in all its Branches'.

> Any Gentleman that please to make Trial will find their Work faithfully executed in the neatest Manner by . . . the above, many years Foreman to the eminent Richard Woods, Land Surveyor and Designer of New Work'.[238]

Both 'gardener' and 'land surveyor' were terms with a range of meanings in the eighteenth century. The former could mean, as today, somebody involved in the practical business of planting, weeding, mowing and the like, either employed permanently by a single individual, or working on a flexible basis for several. But it could also be used for a nurseryman, whose primary business was the supply of trees, shrubs and other plants, some of whom were running large businesses by the 1760s and 1770s. The most important was William Aram, who began operating around 1760, and was joined in business by his son-in-law John Mackie in the 1770s. Their nursery at Lakenham, just outside Norwich, sounds almost like a modern garden centre.[239] The diarist Parson Woodforde made a number of visits there, driving around the grounds in a carriage and ordering shrubs which were delivered to his home at Weston Longville a short time later. Distance was no problem to the company, which appears to have run a mobile pruning service for a time, dealing with gentlemen's fruit trees as far away as Anmer in north-west Norfolk.[240] Other large nurseries included that run by Frederick Fitt from Hoveton from the 1770s, until he went bankrupt in 1793 with a stock described as 'upwards of 20,000 forest and fruit trees, a large quantity of shrubs, greenhouse plants etc.' (all to be sold 'exceedingly cheap, the proprietor being under the necessity of clearing the ground').[241] He provided some of the plants for Richmond's new landscape at Beeston St Lawrence.[242] William Griffin of Mundford, just over the county boundary in Suffolk, also supplied many Norfolk estates, and as we have noted, provided some at least of the trees for the great belt at West Tofts. It is quite possible that some of these men offered advice on designing parks and pleasure grounds. 'Land surveyors' were certainly often involved in such work, not surprisingly given that laying out a park in Brown's style required considerable surveying skills and an ability to deal with levels. The surveyor Joseph Rumball, who prepared the plan in advance of the removal of the walled gardens at Ditchingham in 1764, almost certainly designed the lake and other features there: while John Hare – called in to improve the lake at Kimberley a few years after Brown had worked there – seems to have been primarily a land agent and surveyor.

Many of the new parkland landscapes of the eighteenth century were, in fact, probably designed by the owners themselves, assisted by their head gardeners. Because the new style depended so much on the character of the topography, some of these amateur compositions, such as Bayfield (Figure 135), are arguably more successful expressions of Brown's ideas than either Langley or Melton Constable, where he had to contend with particularly challenging natural conditions.

But it seems unlikely that the landscapes laid out around great mansions like at Raynham or Blickling – both of which underwent major changes in the 'Brown' period – can have been designed solely by their owners and head gardeners, and perhaps improbable that they were the work of local men like Rumball or Gooch. Some, indeed, may have been developed with the guidance of nationally important designers like Richmond or Woods.

Figure 135.
Bayfield Park, north Norfolk. Although it was not designed by Brown, this is one of the most successful landscapes in his style in Norfolk. (Photo: Roger Last, 2011)

Conclusion

Capability Brown may have been responsible for only a handful of landscapes in Norfolk but, as this short volume will hopefully have demonstrated, these are all of considerable interest and, carefully studied, can throw important new light on the wider character of his work. Much remains to be discovered about, in particular, 'shadowy' sites like Buckenham Tofts; but it is doubtful whether many other places in the county will turn out to have been the work of Capability Brown and his able team. The county can, however, boast numerous other landscape parks, designed by Brown's rivals and 'imitators'; by local surveyors and nurserymen; and by owners and their head gardeners. Many of these are creations of immense beauty and importance, just as worthy of our attention. They, too, need to be carefully preserved for the enjoyment of future generations.

ENDNOTES

ABBREVIATIONS
HER   Historic Environment Record, Gressenhall
NRO   Norfolk Record Office
RHS   Royal Horticultural Society

CHAPTER 1.

[1] For a description of Brown's style, see: D. Stroud, *Capability Brown* (1st edn, London, 1950), pp. 27–35. C. Hussey, *English Gardens and Landscapes 1700–1750* (London, 1967); T. Hinde, Capability *Brown: the story of a master gardener* (London, 1986); R. Turner, *Capability Brown and the Eighteenth-Century English Landscape* (Chichester, 1999); J. Brown, *The Omnipotent Magician: Lancelot 'Capability' Brown* (London, 2011); L. Mayer, *Capability Brown and the English Landscape Garden* (Princes Risborough, 2011).

[2] H. Walpole, *The Connoisseur*, Vol. 192, issues 773–4, p. 233.

[3] S. Shields, '"Mr Brown Engineer": Lancelot Brown's early work at Grimsthorpe Castle and Stowe', *Garden History* 34, 2 (2006), pp. 174–91.

[4] J. M. Robinson, *Temples of Delight: Stowe Landscape Gardens* (London, 1999); G. Clarke, 'Grecian taste and gothic virtue: Lord Cobham's gardening programme and its iconography', *Apollo* 97 (1973), pp. 56–67.

[5] *Public Advertiser*, 9 September 1772.

[6] *Public Advertiser*, 9 September 1772.

[7] P. Willis, 'Capability Brown's account with Drummonds Bank, 1753–1783', *Architectural History* 27 (1984), 382–91; J. Gregory, S. Spooner and T. Williamson, 'Lancelot "Capability" Brown: a research impact review', English Heritage Research Report no. 50 (London, 2015).

[8] P. Willis, *Charles Bridgeman and the English Landscape Garden* (2nd edn, London, 2002).

[9] T. Williamson, *The Archaeology of the Landscape Park: garden design in Norfolk, England, c.1680–1840* (Oxford, 1998), pp. 47–96.

[10] T. Mowl, *An Insular Rococo: Architecture, Politics and Society in Ireland and England, 1710–70* (London, 1999), pp. 72–87.

[11] Quoted in T. Richardson, *The Arcadian Friends: inventing the English landscape garden* (London, 2007), p. 125.

[12] Staffordshire Record Office, D240/E(A)/2/133.

[13] The avenues are shown clearly on Andrew Dury and John Andrews' map of Hertfordshire, surveyed in the early 1760s, several years after Brown had finished working here; see A. Macnair, A. Rowe and T. Williamson, *Dury and Andrews' Map of Hertfordshire Society and Landscape in the Eighteenth Century* (Oxford, 2015), pp. 181–2.

[14] Plan of Temple Newsam; West Yorkshire Archives, Leeds, 100/EA/20 5A.

[15] West Sussex Record Office, PHA/6623.

[16] Quoted in Stroud, *Capability Brown*, p. 157.

[17] D. Brown, 'Lancelot Brown and his Associates', *Garden History* 29, 1 (2001) pp. 2–11; D. Brown and T. Williamson, *Lancelot Brown and the Capability Men: landscape revolution in eighteenth-century England* (London, 2016).

[18] Brown, 'Lancelot Brown and his Associates'; Account of Lancelot Brown at Drummond's Bank, RBS Archives.

[19] D. Brown, 'Nathaniel Richmond (1724–1784) – One of the Gentleman Improvers', unpublished PhD thesis (UEA 2000).

[20] Brown, 'Lancelot Brown and his Associates'.

[21] T. Whately, *Observations on Modern Gardening* (London, 1770), p. 148.

[22] W. Roberts, *Memoirs of the Life and Correspondence of Mrs Hannah More* (London, 1836), p. 267.

[23] *Gazetteer and New Daily Advertiser*, 13 December 1780.

[24] E. Burke, *A Philosophical Enquiry into the Origin of our Ideas of the Sublime and the Beautiful* (London, 1756), p. 155.

[25] Whately, *Observations on Modern Gardening*, p. 146.

[26] J. Roberts, 'Well tempered clay: constructing water features in the landscape park', *Garden History* 2, 1 (2001), pp. 12–28.

[27] West Sussex Record Office, PHA/6623; Bowood archives, contact with Lancelot Brown, August 1762.

[28] Roberts, 'Well tempered clay', pp. 17–18.

[29] Chatsworth archives C22, unpaginated; C21, pp. 46–7, 211–15.

[30] A view already well established in the eighteenth century: H. Walpole, *The History of the Modern Taste in Gardening* (London, 1780); S. Bending, 'H. Walpole and eighteenth-century garden history', *Journal of the Warburg and Courtaulds Institutes* 57 (1994), pp. 209–26; S. Bending, 'A natural revolution?', in K. Sharpe and S. Zwicker, *Refiguring Revolutions. Aesthetics and Politics from the English Revolution to the Romantic Revolution* (Berkeley, 1998), pp. 241–66.

[31] B. P. Lange, 'The English garden and patriotic discourse' in H.-J. Diller *et al*, *Englishness* (*Anglistic & Englischunterricht* 46 and 47) (Heidelberg, 1998).

[32] M. Girouard, *The English Town: a history of urban life* (London, 1990), pp. 76–7; Girouard, *Life in the English Country House: a social and architectural history* (London, 1978), pp.189–95.

[33] N. Cossons, *The BP Book of Industrial Archaeology* (London, 1987), pp. 254–8; D. Bogart, 'Did Turnpike Trusts Increase Transportation Investment in Eighteenth-Century England?', *The Journal of Economic History* 65, 2 (2005), pp. 439–68; W. Albert, *The Turnpike Road System in England 1663–1840* (Cambridge, 1972).

[34] S. Tarlow, *The Archaeology of Improvement in Britain, 1750–1860* (Cambridge, 2007).

[35] J. Finch, 'Three men in a boat: biographies and narratives in the historic landscape', *Landscape Research* 33, 5 (2008), pp. 511–30; at p. 516.

[36] J. Barnatt and T. Williamson, *Chatsworth: a landscape history* (Macclesfield, 2005), p. 105.

[37] J. Fletcher, *Gardens of Earthly Delight: the history of deer parks* (Oxford, 2011); R. Liddiard (ed.), *The Medieval Park: new perspectives* (Macclesfield, 2007); S. Mileson, *Parks in Medieval England* (Oxford, 2009).

[38] E. A. Goodwyn, *Selections from Norwich Newspapers, 1760–1790* (Ipswich, 1972), p. 15.

[39] Girouard, *Life in the English Country House*, pp. 119–60.

[40] Girouard, *Life in the English Country House*, pp. 194–203.

[41] Girouard, *Life in the English Country House*, p. 210.

[42] Fletcher, *Gardens of Earthly Delight*, pp. 117–18.

[43] D. Cruikshank, *A Guide to the Georgian Buildings of Britain and Ireland* (London, 1985), pp. 2–23.

[44] A. Smart, *The Life and Art of Allan Ramsay* (London, 1952), p. 93.

[45] D. Irwin, *Neoclassicism* (London, 1997); H. Honour, *Neo-classicism* (London, 1977).

[46] D. Yarwood, *Robert Adam* (London, 1970), pp. 47–87; J. Fleming, *Robert Adam and his Circle in Edinburgh and Rome* (London, 1962), pp. 170–219.

[47] G. Beard, *The Work of Robert Adam* (London, 1992).

[48] C. Gilbert, *The Life and Works of Thomas Chippendale* (London, 1978); R. Reilly, *Josiah Wedgwood 1730–1795* (London, 1992).

[49] Quoted in Stroud, *Capability Brown*, p. 157.

[50] Honour, *Neo-Classicism*, pp. 101–14; A. Forty, *Objects of Desire: design and society since 1750* (London, 1986), p. 24.

[51] Honour, *Neoclassicism*, p. 13.

[52] H. Cook and T. Williamson (eds), *Water Management in the English Landscape: field, marsh and meadow* (Edinburgh, 1999).

[53] J. Armstrong, *The Art of Preserving Health: a poem* (London, 1744), pp. 10–20.

[54] L. Dickens and M. Stanton, *An Eighteenth-Century Correspondence: being the letters of Deane Swift – Pitt – the Lytteltons and the Grenvilles – Lord Dacre – Robert Nugent – Charles Jenkinson – the Earls of Guildford, Coventry, & Hardwicke – Sir Edward Turner – Mr. Talbot of Lacock, and others to Sanderson Miller, Esq., of Radway* (London, 1910), p. 416.

[55] Cossens, *Industrial Archaeology*, pp. 244–5.

[56] A. Ingram, *Horse-drawn Vehicles Since 1760* (Blandford, 1977).

CHAPTER 2.

[57] W. White, *History, Gazetteer and Directory of Norfolk* (Sheffield, 1864) p. 584.

[58] F. Blomefield, *An Essay Towards a Topographical History of Norfolk* (London, 1805), Vol. II, p. 541.

[59] C. Rawcliffe, 'Wodehouse, John', in S. Roskell and L. Clark (eds), *The History of Parliament: The House of Commons 1386–1421*, http://www.historyofparliamentonline.org [accessed 8 May 2016].

[60] Blomefield, *Topographical History,* Vol. II, p. 540.

[61] Blomefield, *Topographical History*, Vol. II, p. 537.

[62] Blomefield, *Topographical History*, Vol. II, pp. 543–5.

[63] T. Wotton, E. Kimber and R. Johnson, *The Baronetage of England*, 3 Vols (London, 1771), Vol. I, pp. 73, 78–9.

[64] P. A. W. Dallas, 'Elite Landscapes in Late Medieval and Early Modern East Anglia: Families, Residences and the Development of Exclusivity' (unpublished PhD thesis, University of East Anglia, 2013), p. 292.

[65] Dallas, 'Elite Landscape', p. 234.

[66] Blomefield, *Topographical History,* Vol. II, p. 552.

[67] Dallas, 'Elite Landscapes', pp. 292–4.

[68] J. Chambers, *A General History of the County of Norfolk, Intended to Convey all the Information of a Norfolk Tour* (Norwich, 1829), Vol. I, p. 348.

[69] Blomefield, *Topographical History*, Vol. II, p. 544.

[70] H. Colvin, *A Biographical Dictionary of British Architects, 1600–1840*, 4th edn (New Haven and London, 2008), pp. 1009–10.

[71] J. Harris, *William Talman: maverick architect* (London, 1982), pp. 40–1.

[72] Harris, *William Talman*, p. 40.

[73] Harris, *William Talman*, p. 41.

[74] Blomefield, *Topographical History*, Vol. II, p. 506.

[75] Blomefield, *Topographical History*, Vol. II, p. 539.

[76] R. Sedgewick, 'Wodehouse, Armine', in R. Sedgewick (ed.), *The History of Parliament: The House of Commons 1714–7754–1790,* http://www.historyofparliamentonline.org [Accessed 2 May 2016].

[77] Letter from Armine Wodehouse to Lord Townshend, NRO: BL/T 8/6/132–151.

[78] J. P. Neale, *Views of the Seats of Noblemen and Gentlemen in England, Scotland, Wales and Ireland* (London, 1818–23), Vol. III, 1820, 'Kimberley Hall'.

[79] Designs for the interiors of Kimberley dated 1770 are held in the RIBA Drawings Collection.

[80] N. Pevsner and B. Wilson, *The Buildings of England: Norfolk 2: North-West and South* (New Haven and London, 2002), pp. 510–11.

[81] A. M. F. Pickard, 'An eighteenth century building campaign: the improvements at Kimberley Hall, 1755-1758 commissioned by Sir Armine Wodehouse, Bart., a preliminary study' (unpublished MA thesis, UEA, 1997), pp. 8–10.

[82] Letter from Thomas Prowse to Sir Armine, 1 October 1755, NRO KIM 8/1/1.

[83] Neale, Vol. III, 'Kimberley Hall'.

[84] NRO KIM 8/1/2.

[85] Pickard, 'An eighteenth-century building campaign', p. 67.

86 The account book of Lancelot Brown, RHS Lindley Library.

[87] J. Grigor, *The Eastern Arboretum: or a register of remarkable trees, seats, gardens etc in the County of Norfolk* (London and Norwich, 1841), p. 275.

[88] *The Gentleman's Magazine*, n.s. 2, September 1834, pp. 313–14.

[89] J. Abercrombie, *The Hot House Gardener* (London, 1789), p. 133.

[90] Chambers, *General History of the County of Norfolk*, Vol. I, p. 349.

[91] Grigor, *Eastern Arboretum*, pp. 275, 277.

[92] Grigor, *Eastern Arboretum*, p. 274.

[93] NRO KIM 5/1/3.

[94] Expenses of building Carlton Bridge, NRO KIM 6/13.

[95] List of timber on the Kimberley Estates, NRO KIM/8/3/1.

[96] J. Allibone, *Anthony Salvin: pioneer of Gothic Revival architecture 1799–1881* (Columbia, 1987), p. 160.

[97] Grigor, *Eastern Arboretum*, pp. 275–6.

[98] In 1833–6 Salvin worked at North Runcton Hall for David Gurney and Nesfield provided a plan for the layout of the gardens. Allibone, *Anthony Salvin*, p. 159.

[99] S. R. Evans, *Masters of their Craft: the art, architecture and garden design of the Nesfields* (Cambridge, 2014), p. 173.

[100] A. Hawkins and J. Powell (eds), *The Journal of John Wodehouse, First Earl of Kimberley for 1862–1902* (Camden Soc. Fifth Series, Vol. 9, London, 1997), p. 2.

[101] J. D. Andrews, 'How a 'noble' legend stemmed from a common noun' (unpublished manuscript, 1974), p. 13. Copy in Historic England's listing file for Kimberley Hall.

[102] Pevsner and Wilson, *Norfolk* 2, p. 458.

CHAPTER 3.

[103] F. Blomefield, *An Essay Towards a Topographical History of the County of Norfolk*, Vol. X (London, 1809), pp. 147–52, on http://www.british-history.ac.uk/topographical-hist-

norfolk/vol10/ accessed 17 November 2015.

[104] http://www.historyofparliamentonline.org/volume/16901715/member/berney-richard-1674-1738, accessed 5 February 2016.

[105] The Berney coat of arms may be seen on the south parapet of the church tower.

[106] http://www.historyofparliamentonline.org/volume/16901715/member/berney-richard-1674-1738, accessed 5 February 2016.

[107] NRO, Beauchamp-Proctor collection BEA9/7, dated c.1738.

[108] NRO, Beauchamp-Proctor collection MF/RO124/9, no.138, advice from John Southgate dated 24 February 1738.

[109] NRO, Beauchamp-Proctor collection BEA10/92, letter from John Lows to George Proctor, 24 February 1738.

[110] Norfolk HER 49547.

[111] N. Pevsner and B. Wilson, *The Buildings of England: Norfolk 2: North-West and South* (New Haven and London, 2002), p. 511.

[112] J. H. W. Jevons of Langley School in a letter to *Country Life* dated 10 March 1960.

[113] W. Robinson, *The History and Antiquities of Tottenham* (London, 1840), pp. 124–7.

[114] The B-P arms were then for Proctor first and fourth argent, a chevron between three martlets sable, and for Beauchamp second and third gules, a fess between six billets (three and three barways), or, a canton ermine, for Beauchamp. Crest, on a mount vert, greyhound sejant argent, spotted brown, collared or; motto: *toujours fideles*. As described by W. Betham, *The Baronetage of England*, Vol. III (London, 1803).

[115] 'Plain Common Freeholder', *Letters to Sir William Beauchamp-Proctor*, a pamphlet published in 1768, pp. 16–17.

[116] J. Harris, *The Artist and the Country House* (London, 1979), p. 225.

[117] J. Maddison, unpublished paper, 'Some Notes on the Architecture of Langley Park', 1993, Langley School Archive, p. 1.

[118] Pevsner and Wilson, *Norfolk* 2, p. 511.

[119] The drawing for this design is at the Victoria and Albert Museum, Collection PDP, Museum Number E.2678-1948.

[120] Bills from these cabinet-makers are to be found in NRO, BEA305/71, 305/79 and 305/45.

[121] Bills for commissions were not presented very promptly, particularly for regular clients. The dining chairs itemised in NRO, BEA305/71, 305/79.

[122] D. Stroud, *Capability Brown* (London, 1975), p. 231.

[123] NRO BEA MF/RO 205/2 (140) Map of Langley Park by L.B., 1765.

[124] http://www.historyofparliamentonline.org/volume/1754-1790/member/beauchamp-proctor-sir-william-1722-73, accessed 6 March 2016.

[125] J. C. Hampp was the merchant, see Pevsner and Wilson, *Norfolk 2*, p. 70.

[126] L. H. M. Hill 'The Custances and their Family Circle', *Parson Woodforde Society Quarterly Journal* No. 3 (1970), pp. 44–5 quoted in R. Wilson and A. Mackley, *Creating Paradise: the building of the English country house 1660–1880* (Cambridge, 2000), pp. 333–4.

[127] L. Bethany, *Edward Jerningham and his Friends: a series of eighteenth century letters* (London, 1919) letter: Mary Beauchamp-Proctor to Edward Jerningham, dated 24 June 1781, p. 125.

[128] Bethany, *Edward Jerningham and his Friends,* letter dated January 1783, p. 122.

[129] Bethany, *Edward Jerningham and his Friends,* letter dated 19 August 1783, p. 125.

[130] J. P. Neale, *Views of the Seats of Noblemen and Gentlemen*, Vol. III (London, 1818–23), pp. 726–8.

[131] Bethany, *Edward Jerningham and his Friends*, letter dated 24 June 1781, p. 120.

[132] Soane's Museum Drawings, Ledger A, 15 March 1788, notes by Jill Lever in 2009, on jeromeonline.co.uk, accessed 20 March 2016.

[133] Letter from Lord Hardwicke to George III's Windsor comptroller, in A. Aspinall (ed.), *The Later Correspondence of George III*, Vol. II, *1793–7* (Cambridge,1963), pp. 276–7.

[134] Bethany, *Edward Jerningham and his Friends*, letter dated 3 September 1789, p. 137.

[135] Bethany, *Edward Jerningham and his Friends*, letter dated 13 August 1812, p. 136.

[136] Langley Estate map of 1816, Norfolk Records Office, ref. NRO DS157.

[137] J. Grigor, *The Eastern Arboretum: or a register of remarkable trees, seats, gardens etc in the County of Norfolk* (London and Norwich, 1841), p. 266.

[138] Grigor, *Eastern Arboretum*, pp. 267–8.

[139] www.heritage.norfolk.gov.uk, NHER 10326, accessed 30 March 2016.

[140] O. Brackett, 'Langley Park, Norfolk', *Country Life* 2 July 1927, pp. 16-22.

CHAPTER 4.

[141] Melton Constable Conservation Area – final draft 2008 North Norfolk County Council http://www.northnorfolk.org/files/MeltonConstableCA_final08.pdf

[142] Norfolk Historic Environment Record, Norfolk County Council, Gressenhall, East Dereham. St Peter's Church ref: NHER 3247, Crop Marks ref: NHER 3228, http://www.heritage.norfolk.gov.uk//search-results

[143] W. White, *History, Gazetteer and Directory of Norfolk* (Sheffield, 1845), p. 744.

[144] O. Rackham, *Trees and Woodland in the British Landscape* (London, 1976), p. 150.

[145] Anon., 'Melton Constable, Norfolk . . . the Seat of Lord Hastings', *Country Life*, 16 September 1905, p. 384

[146] Norfolk Historic Environment Record, Norfolk County Council, Gressenhall, East Dereham. Medieval moated site ref: NHER 3229, http://www.heritage.norfolk.gov.uk//search-results

[147] D. Astley, 'Astleys of Melton Constable 1235–1936', unpublished typescript, Norwich Millennium Library Locals Studies.

[148] Astley, 'Astleys of Melton Constable'.

[149] D. Yaxley, 'An Introduction to the Astley Family', in R. W. Ketton-Cremer, *Three Generations: based on letters of the Astley family during the Civil War. With additional material on the Astleys and Melton Constable (*Dereham, 1992), p. i.

[150] R. W. Ketton-Cremer, *Norfolk in the Civil War* (Norwich, 1985), pp. 163–4.

[151] Ketton-Cremer, *Three Generations*, p. 22.

[152] The Peerage website, http://www.thepeerage.com/p12655.htm#i126550

[153] J. Kenworthy-Browne, P. Reid, M. Sayer and D. Watkin, *Burke's and Savills Guide to Country Houses, Vol 3: East Anglia* (London, 1981), pp. 157–158.

[154] G. Winkley, *Country Houses of Norfolk* (Lowestoft, 1986), pp. 104–5.

[155] T. Williamson and A. Taigel, *Gardens in Norfolk* (Norwich, 1990), p. 33.

[156] A. Taigel and T. Williamson, 'Some early geometric gardens in Norfolk', *Journal of Garden History* 11 (Parts 1 and 2) (1991), p. 78.

[157] Yaxley, 'Introduction to the Astley Family', pp. 35–7.

[158] Yaxley, 'Introduction to the Astley family', pp. 35–7.

[159] The Peerage website, http://www.thepeerage.com/p12658.htm

[160] '1799 Inventory of Contents of Melton Constable Hall', part of uncatalogued Astley papers from Seaton Delaval), Norfolk Record Office ref: ACC 2013/217.

[161] J. Brown, *Lancelot 'Capability' Brown: the omnipotent magician, 1716–1718* (London, 2011), p. 155.

[162] M. Armstrong, *The History and Antiquities of the County of Norfolk*, Vol. VII (Norwich, 1781), p. 84.

[163] Brown, *Lancelot 'Capability' Brown*, p. 182.

[164] T. Williamson, *The Archaeology of the Landscape Park: garden design in Norfolk, England, 1680–1840* (British Archaeological Report, British Series 268, Oxford, 1998), p. 108.

[165] D. Stroud, *Capability Brown* (London, 1950), p. 121.

[166] E. Hyams, *Capability Brown and Humphrey Repton* (London, 1971), p. 56.

[167] Williamson, *Archaeology of the Landscape Park*, pp. 107–8.

[168] Brown, *Lancelot 'Capability' Brown*, pp. 217 and 287.

[169] Armstrong, *The History and Antiquities of the County of Norfolk*, Vol. VII, p. 83.

[170] A. Young, *The Farmer's Tour through the East of England*, Vol. II (London, 1771), p. 62.

[171] Williamson, *Archaeology of the Landscape Park*, p. 108.

[172] J. Chambers, *A General History of the County of Norfolk*, Vol. II (Norwich, 1829), pp. 784-5.

[173] Melton Constable, 1784 Road Closure orders, NRO C/Sce 2/2/11.

[174] Chambers, *A General History*, p. 784.

[175] Williamson, *Archaeology of the Landscape Park*, pp. 262–3.

[176] S. Bate, 'Lancelot "Capability" Brown didn't build any kitchen gardens in Norfolk – or did he?' (Norfolk Gardens Trust *News*, Autumn Edition, 2015), pp. 4–7 (digital copy: www.norfolkgt.org.uk).

[177] 1729–40 Letters to Sir Hans Sloane, British Library Manuscript Collections, Sloane 4078, f.66.

[178] M. Drummond, 'Sir Edward Astley', in L. Namier and J. Brooke (eds), *The History of Parliament: The House of Commons 1754–1790* (London, 1964): http://www.historyofparliamentonline.org/volume/1754-1790/member/astley-sir-edward-1729–1802.

[179] Williamson, *Archaeology of the Landscape Park*, p. 108.

[180] J. Neville, 'Briningham Belle Vue smock mill', Norfolk Mills Website 2006, http://www.norfolkmills.co.uk/Windmills/briningham-belle-vue-smockmill

[181] Armstrong, The *History and Antiquities of the County of Norfolk*, Vol. VII, p. 84.

[182] M. Drummond, 'Sir Edward Astley', in L. Namier and J. Brooke (eds), *The History of Parliament: The House of Commons 1754–1790* (London, 1964): http://www.historyofparliamentonline.org/volume/1754-1790/member/astley-sir-edward-1729-1802.

[183] Parks and Gardens UK website, Melton Constable Hall, http://www.parksandgardens.org/places-and-people/site/2261/history

[184] J. Grigor, *The Eastern Arboretum: or a register of remarkable trees, seats, gardens etc in the County of Norfolk* (London and Norwich, 1841), pp. 190–1.

[185] Anon., 'Melton Constable, Norfolk . . . the Seat of Lord Hastings', Country *Life*, 16 September 1905, p. 380.

[186] National Railway Museum website, 'Original plans for the building of Melton Constable railway works and village' pdf ref: http://www.nrm.org.uk/~/media/Files/NRM/PDF/archiveslists2012/railwaycompanyworks/Introduction%20to%20Plaistow%20Works%20drawing%20list.pdf

CHAPTER 5.

[187] L. Schmidt, C. Keller and P. Feversham, *Holkham* (Munich, 2005), pp. 81–102.

[188] Holkham Hall archives, A/11, A/32, A/34, A/35, and A/37.

[189] Holkham Hall archives, A/37, A/38, A/39; T. Williamson, *The Archaeology of the Landscape Park: garden design in Norfolk, England, 1680–1840* (British Archaeological Report, British Series 268, Oxford, 1998), pp. 67–70.

[190] H. Repton, *Sketches and Hints on Landscape Gardening* (London, 1796), p. 328.

[191] NRO C/Sce 1, Road Order Book 1, pp. 441–7; pp. 505–8.

[192] Holkham Hall archives, A/46.

[193] K. Goodway, 'William Emes and the Flower Garden at Sandon, Staffordshire', *Garden History* 24, 1 (1996), pp. 24–9.

[194] Holkham Hall archives, A/46; N. Antram and G. Jackson-Stops, *Kedleston Hall, Derbyshire* (London, 1988), pp. 65–8.

[195] *The Times*, 12 April 1794.

[196] Holkham Hall archives, A/47; Holkham Hall library Humphry Repton Red Book, 1789.

[197] Williamson, *Archaeology of the Landscape Park*, p. 104; NRO PD 679/14.

[198] NRO MC3 252 (A) 466 X 4).

[199] Holkham Hall archives.

[200] R. Turner, *Capability Brown and the Eighteenth-Century English Landscape* (Stroud, 1999), p. 192.

[201] W. S. Gilpin, *Practical Hints upon Landscape Gardening* (London, 1832), p. 86.

[202] Gilpin, *Practical Hints*, p. 186.

[203] P. Willis, *Charles Bridgeman* (London, 2002), pp. 85, 185, and plate 80b.

[204] Wolterton Hall archives, Wolt 8/21; Williamson, *Archaeology of the Landscape Park*, pp. 77–8.

[205] NRO S175B.

[206] Wolterton Hall archives, Wolt 8/68.

[207] P. Dallas, R. Last and T. Williamson, *Norfolk Gardens and Designed Landscapes* (Oxford, 2013), pp. 425–8.

[208] N. Pevsner, *North-West and South Norfolk* (London, 1962), p. 135.

[209] J. Brown, *Lancelot 'Capability' Brown: the omnipotent magician* (London, 2011), p. 181.

[210] Norfolk Millennium Library, Ditchingham file.

[211] NRO 1761/2.

[212] NRO MC 166/203, 632X5; private collection.

[213] NRO NCR Case 16e/108.

[214] T. Williamson, I. Ringwood, and S. Spooner, *Lost Country Houses of Norfolk: history, archaeology and myth* (Woodbridge, 2015), pp. 110–14, 264.

[215] NRO PTR 3/3 758 X1; Dallas *et al*, *Norfolk Gardens and Designed Landscapes*, pp. 102–3.

[216] NRO PTR 3/6 758 X1.

[217] NRO PTR 3/47 2; NRO C/Sce 1/3.

218 NRO PTR 3/47 1.

219 D. Brown and T. Williamson, *Lancelot Brown and Capability Men: landscape revolution in eighteenth-century England* (London, 2016), pp. 141–2; D. Brown, 'Nathaniel Richmond (1724–1784) – One of the Gentleman Improvers', unpublished PhD thesis (UEA 2000).

220 British Library, Ordnance Survey drawings, 1821, sheet 251.

221 NRO MC 77/1/521/7.

222 N. Kent, *General View of the Agriculture of the County of Norfolk* (London, 1794), p. 41.

223 Sales catalogue, 1780: NRO MC 77/1/521/7.

CHAPTER 6.

224 H. Repton, *Sketches and Hints on Landscape Gardening* (London, 1795), p. 110; H. Repton, *An Inquiry into the Changes in Taste in Landscape Gardening* (London, 1806), p. 328.

225 Brown and Williamson, *Capability Men*, pp. 142–5.

226 Marylebone Archives, Deed 456. Richmond countersigned the existing lease between William Henry Portman and William Baker. Richmond is first rated at Marylebone for 'Houses and Land' in 1759.

227 Bristol University Library, Letter, Humphry Repton to Revd Norton Nicholls, 26 August 1788.

228 For the house, see N. Wright, 'The Gentry and their Houses in Norfolk and Suffolk c.1550–1859' (unpublished PhD, University of East Anglia, 1990); and J. Haslam, 'Beeston Hall', *Country Life* 172 (1983), pp. 270–4. The edge of the park is shown on a map connected with a road diversion, carried out by *writ of ad quod damnum* in 1756: NRO Castle Museum deposit 30/1/73 T 190 a.

229 NRO MC 36/136 480X; the letter is in a private collection.

230 F. Cowell, *Richard Woods (1715–1793): Master of the Pleasure Ground* (Woodbridge, 2009).

231 Brown and Williamson, *Capability Men*, p. 119.

232 NRO NRS 21369.

233 NRO NRS 8379 24D.

234 NRO DN/TA 37.

235 NRO NRS 8379 24D.

236 *Norwich Mercury*, 4 June 1747.

237 *Norwich Mercury*, 26 January 1752.

238 *Norwich Mercury*, 4 February 1764.

239 Williamson, *Archaeology of the Landscape Park*, pp. 170–1.

240 R. L. Winstanley, *Parson Woodforde: Diary of the First Six Norfolk Years* (London, 1984), p. 76; NRO MC 40/115-126.

241 *Norwich Mercury*, 11 February 1793.

242 NRO MC 36/136 480X.

Index

Entries in bold refer to the Figures